The Five Elements

UNDERSTAND YOURSELF AND ENHANCE YOUR RELATIONSHIPS WITH THE WISDOM OF THE WORLD'S OLDEST PERSONALITY TYPE SYSTEM

DONDI DAHLIN

FOREWORD BY DONNA EDEN
AFTERWORD BY TITANYA DAHLIN

A TARCHERPERIGEE BOOK

tarcherperigee

An imprint of Penguin Random House LLC
375 Hudson Street
New York, New York 10014

Photography by Narrative Images Photography: www.narrativeimagesphoto.com

Tarcher and Perigee are registered trademarks, and the colophon is a trademark of Penguin Random House LLC.

Most TarcherPerigee books are available at special quantity discounts for bulk purchase for sales promotions, premiums, fund-raising, and educational needs. Special books or book excerpts also can be created to fit specific needs. For details, write: SpecialMarkets@penguinrandomhouse.com.

LIBRARY OF CONGRESS CATALOGING-IN-PUBLICATION DATA
Names: Dahlin, Dondi, author.
Title: The five elements : understand yourself and enhance your relationships with the wisdom of the world's oldest personality type system / by Dondi Dahlin ; foreword by Donna Eden ; afterword by Titanya Dahlin.
Description: New York : TarcherPerigee, 2016.
Identifiers: LCCN 2016018138 (print) | LCCN 2016035084 (ebook) | ISBN 9780399176296 (paperback) | ISBN 9781101993286
Subjects: LCSH: Personality. | Self-actualization (Psychology) | Happiness. | Five agents (Chinese philosophy) | BISAC: BODY, MIND & SPIRIT / Inspiration & Personal Growth. | SELF-HELP / Personal Growth / Happiness.
Classification: LCC BF698 .D636 2016 (print) | LCC BF698 (ebook) | DDC 155.2/6—dc23

Printed in the United States of America
7th Printing

Book design by Pauline Neuwirth

I dedicate this book to my father, Raymond "Don" Dahlin, who was a Wood/Fire/Water. As a conservative agnostic Republican, he would have thought this book was "entertaining, but not science," and he still would have supported me to write it. His name is a part of my name and I inherited his Wood, which helped me get this book written and reach my goals. My Water tries to make sense of his death every day of my life.

◼

I love you, Dad. I am two halves of you and Mom— two of the most charismatic and incredible human beings the world has ever known.

◼

I am blessed.

◼

CONTENTS

Foreword

NOTHING MAKES IT MORE clear that we are each a unique combination of inner forces than having a second child. For me, it started during pregnancy. My first child, Tanya, seemed the model of sweet gentleness. She never kicked. It was as if she was tuned into my needs and wanted to adapt to them. When I would lie down, she would softly roll in ways that accommodated my new position. Even her sleep patterns matched mine. I expected my second pregnancy to be similar. I was in for a stormy surprise! For starters, Dondi's sleep patterns never matched mine. As I was dozing off, her tiny hands would start moving in ways that were strong and deliberate. I used to joke that I had a little basketball player who loved to dribble in there. Rather than trying to accommodate my needs, it was clear that this baby already had her own agenda, a distinct individuality that would not be tamed by being so tiny and confined in a tight dark space.

In trying to figure out how two daughters who draw from the same gene pool and even have the same astrological sign (they were born three years apart on the same day, September 30) could be so unalike, I have had the benefit of being able to draw from so many psychological and spiritual systems that try to make sense of human differences. None has been more useful to me than the most ancient of all of them, the Chinese Five Element theory, which Dondi—the one who wouldn't be tamed—beautifully explains in this book.

Understanding the Five Elements is like having a pair of special glasses that allows you to peer into the deep workings of what you can see on the surface. You can witness two people flowing together like a team or fighting like enemies, but that gives you little insight into what is driving them. The Five Element system gives you this insight.

The Five Elements were mapped more than two thousand years ago by Chinese physicians who categorized all of life into "five elements" or "five phases" or "five seasons." This model was the basis for understanding how the world works, how societies organize themselves, and what the human body needs to maintain health. It is an elegant framework for sympathetically appreciating human character, temperament, cycles, and illnesses.

The book you are holding offers a wonderful introduction to this profoundly sophisticated system, providing an overview of each of the Five Elements so you can begin to identify your own primary element (or combination), identify the elements of others, and learn how this understanding can bring you greater balance, effectiveness, and happiness within your own life.

The name of the Chinese system is often translated as the "Five Elements" because the ancient pictograms depicted the familiar, concrete, and observable—the elements of Water, Wood, Fire, Earth, and Metal. But don't be fooled. As you will see in this dynamic book, the system has always concentrated on natural *processes*, not on nature in her static forms (the literal

x

translation is "the five walks" or "the five moves"). As Dondi makes clear, the element of Water corresponds with the season of winter, Wood with spring, Fire with summer, Earth with the time of the solstice or equinox, and Metal with autumn.

While each of us contains all five elements, one of them, or a particular combination of two or three, will be more dominant. You will vibrate more easily with people, environments, and activities whose element corresponds with your own. Those that do not will be more challenging for you, but potentially more enriching as their influence expands you.

I started teaching my daughters the Five Elements in their teens and more indirectly exposed them to these teachings when they were younger, as a way to understand people and even thrive in this world. I had seen the energy of the elements in people my whole life and I felt five distinctive personalities from people. And even though I was teaching energy systems and energy medicine since 1977, I didn't learn thoroughly about the actual system of the Chinese Five Elements until I studied with a master acupuncturist, Nancy Post, in 1988, who teaches how to use the Five Elements strategically in the workplace. Nancy gave me the terms Water, Wood, Fire, Earth, and Metal for the energies I had always felt. The Five Elements soon became the most common and interesting conversation in our household. I was impressed by Dondi's grasp of how useful the system can be when, during her twenties, she integrated it with her strong interest in theater and film—she and her sister would analyze a production according to the elements of the characters and the elements of the actors or actresses playing those characters. They could lucidly discuss what the performer had to do to separate from their own element in order to capture the element of the role being played. These were fascinating discussions that showed an incredibly deep understanding of the Five Elements. And you get to benefit from all that analysis because the book discusses the elements of various well-known people to illustrate some of its key principles.

Two very different aspects of human experience are explained by the elements, which is what makes it such an exquisite system. First is your basic nature. Each person's energies are characterized by one of the elements or a personal blend of two or three of them. Second is that in the human life cycle, we travel through periods or phases that are analogous to the elements—or the seasons of nature—in tempo, intensity, and function, each potentially lasting for years. What is remarkable, as you will discover in this book, is that the very same lens, the template provided by the Five Element system, gives profound insight into each of these divergent aspects of the human journey.

So how did Dondi, the embryonic basketball player, come to write this book? In the womb, she was showing the qualities of the Wood element. Woods are deliberate. Their individual expression won't be suppressed. They are forces to be reckoned with. Rather than rolling with the punches, they punch back. And sure enough, as an adult, Dondi has many of the qualities of a strong Wood element. But these qualities were not evident in her childhood. However much she had all the signs of being a Wood while in my belly, her early years were characterized by Earth element and Water element. Remember, we each contain all five elements. The element that dominates at a particular moment in time, while always reflecting your basic nature, may be strongly influenced by the situation or by where you are in your life cycle.

Dondi's Wood element did express itself in qualities of fairness and equanimity, though mostly it was her Earth element that expressed itself in her early years in a sweet, emotional, compassionate, and kind child. But perhaps because she was also the smallest and one of the youngest of all the cousins who played together, she exhibited the Water element (the first element in the cycle, and thus appropriate for the youngest) in sometimes being prone to whining and feeling sorry for herself. But neither whining nor always being sweet was working very well for her, and by the time she was eleven, her other Wood qualities, which had seemed to lie dormant since she was born, came to the forefront. Almost overnight, she became decisive, logical, and determined.

These potentials were always there, as I knew from my pregnancy with her, but for them to be activated, they seemed to require that situations arise in her life that called for Wood qualities. For example, Dondi's room was always a mess. Then one day she tackled her room and cleaned it completely. She dusted, vacuumed, folded clothes, and put everything in its proper place. That day, she announced to the family: "I've cleaned my room, and it will never be messy again!" Now, more than thirty years later, she still keeps a meticulous living environment. She kept to her commitment—she was never messy again. That is the determination of a Wood.

With that determination came an ability to excel. In college, she took first place in the United States in expository speaking. Her interest in acting led to a coveted membership in the Screen Actors Guild and prominent stage and film parts, where she applied her knowledge of the elements. She fought for two years to get her house historically designated and even defended her house in court—a role that is usually reserved for lawyers and historical preservationists. She also loved dance and stood out as a professional dancer and teacher of both Polynesian and Middle Eastern dance forms, ultimately dancing for royalty in the Middle East, celebrities in the United States, and winning the prestigious global Belly Dancer of the Universe competition. Her dance background was one of the many ways she came to understand and apply the Five Element system, having developed with her sister an amazing class that teaches the Five Elements through belly dance. In each day of this five-day class, which Dondi and Tanya have been teaching for nearly two decades in distinguished settings such as the Omega Institute, students immerse themselves in one of the elements and learn about the rhythms, music, costuming, history, culture, and belly dance movements that express that element.

Because Dondi and Tanya grew up with me immersed in the Five Elements, the system is in their bones. And so I am also pleased that Tanya has contributed the Afterword to Dondi's book, and I am deeply honored and proud to be providing this Foreword. You are in for a treat.

Donna Eden
April 2016
Waikoloa, Hawaii

My Life with the Five Elements

MY FRIEND KELLY HAD been trying to find love on singles' websites. She told me that there are lots of questions on matchmaking sites about likes, dislikes, desires, and a person's job and family that don't really tell you much about the person. For instance, singles' Web sites certainly don't tell you how the person behaves under stress. This may be the most important key to a relationship and is probably the biggest reason for breakups and divorce—because people behave differently when under stress, and many times they cannot see eye to eye. Kelly said, "I wish I could just go onto one of these sites, say that I am primarily a Water/Earth type, and have everyone know what that means. Then I would find my soul mate much quicker and we would undoubtedly stay together for the rest of our lives!"

· · ·

Gain Confidence and Clarity with the Help of an Ancient System

The Five Elements have been a part of my daily life since I was a teenager. My mom raised me and my sister to navigate life by understanding how Water, Wood, Fire, Earth, and Metal manifest in the world and in people, and this understanding has truly helped me become who I am today. I have learned how to have patience, understanding, and compassion for people when stress, anger, and frustration could have gotten the best of me. My deep knowledge of this system has strengthened my ability to get along with others instead of letting the nitty-gritty details of life bog me down. It has helped me to negotiate tricky situations in work and uncomfortable phases in relationships and to find a deep and lasting confidence in myself.

Growing Up with the Five Elements

My mother, Donna Eden, taught me and my sister the Five Elements when we were young. She said they would never fail us. As a world-renowned healer who can see energies in the body—darkness and light, flowing (wellness) and not flowing (illness)—she knew what she was talking about. My mom has a kind of X-ray vision that allows her to see not just the vibrations and energy of peoples' bodies down to their organs and bones, but also the vibrations and energy of their hearts and souls. She cannot remember when she didn't see, feel, know, and experience people's "rhythms" and their primary elements of Water, Wood, Fire, Earth, and Metal. Later, as an adult, she encountered teachers who taught her the formal Five Element system that is described in ancient Chinese medical texts and is fundamental to traditional Chinese medicine. Only then did she realize what she had always been experiencing. Today, Mom teaches Eden Energy Medicine all over the world, a healing method developed by her based on nine energy systems in the body. The Five Elements is one of those systems.

These days, my sister and I both work closely with our mom as she travels internationally giving workshops to teach and heal people. But when I became a teenager and young woman, I was often perplexed by how different the three of us were from one another. Our mom was born with a double blessing but also a spiritual burden: Not only can she heal people—and feels that she was born to heal people—but she also is an Earth/Fire combination. Strong Earth types are pulled deep from their core to serve people and will give up everything to make sure people are happy and that peace resides in their hearts. If Earths are not devoting their time to making people feel good, life just doesn't feel right. Taking care of themselves always comes second. Like Earths, Fires also love people, and they love feeling joy and pleasure. If they can recruit everyone around them to feel the same joy that they feel, then life is wonderful.

But this pressing need to give, help, and heal has a downside, too. Mom's urgency to comfort and help people comes from a deeply spiritual place that she has had since she was born, and it cannot just be turned off by logic. Mom would take needy people into our home and give them money, food, and whatever else they asked for, even if they were total strangers and even though we didn't have much money to begin with. As a teenager, I started to move strongly into my Wood element, and I found myself angry and frustrated. I was starting to form the strong opinions that typically come with being a Wood. One of

3

those opinions was that people needed to take responsibility for themselves. Plus, in the early eighties we were living on food stamps and government-issue cheese blocks, so how could we take total strangers into our home and give them our precious food?

When I was young, I didn't understand my mom's Earth/Fire. As a Wood, my tendency was to think that people who do good should be rewarded and people who don't should be punished. As I came to understand the Five Elements better, I realized that it is actually torture for Earths not to help others. They simply cannot bear the pain of seeing someone suffer or struggle. I have seen Earth types (my mom included) wither and weaken if their ability to serve people or animals is curbed or hampered in any way. My mom and the Five Elements taught me that it is not fair to stand in judgment or to see the world in black and white—ever.

Growing up, I also saw that my friends didn't have a system like the Five Elements to explain or depersonalize normal but challenging life events. We were all experiencing our parent's divorces, peer pressure, the confusing surges of hormones, and first romantic relationships. When parents started divorcing—as mine had done—my friends would cry at school. They seemed lost. Divorce is never pain-free, but I seemed to have more space in myself to accept my parents' divorce because I was familiar with the Five Elements. I understood that my mom's Earth and my dad's Wood were at odds (see the Button Pushers, pages 233–35). When my dad was angry or even enraged, I saw that he was a stressed-out Wood/Fire. When my mom was emotional and panicking, I saw that she was a stressed out Earth/Fire. Not only were they from different generations with different values, but their elements were different, and because of this they weren't able to resonate with each other and be a healthy couple together.

Are You Balanced or Imbalanced?

In this book, we talk about balance and imbalance and what it means to be a balanced Water, Wood, Fire, Earth, or Metal. Simply put, balance is the harmony of your body and mind. To have balance is to not be saddled with chemical, emotional, mental, spiritual, or psychological issues. It is to have wholeness, harmony, and joy in the mind, body, and spirit. Imbalance might be repressed emotions or a physical illness that is limiting the full potential of your personality and your authentic self, to shine.

In each phase of my life, the Five Elements have showed me that other people's imbalance has little to do with me. It's not a comment on my worth or even their feelings for me. I can still care for them and make clearheaded choices. For instance, when a dear friend decided that she would end our friendship because I didn't have time to do daily meditation with her, I understood that it was her Metal out of balance. Metals have a lot of need for reverence, and if you don't share their cherished ideas and standards, on their terms, they can get put off. My busy life simply didn't allow me to revere her the way she required. Because I am familiar with the Metal element, I didn't take her decision personally. Similarly, when I once spent time with a friend who scheduled the entire day with bike rides, walks, and exercise, followed by parties all night, I knew this was her Fire energy, not a test to see how much endurance I had. If I hadn't known the elements, I might have assumed that she was competing with me. When a Water boyfriend went into a place of self-pity where I seemed to have no impact, instead of thinking it was about me, I understood that this is often what imbalanced Waters do. When my Wood father was incredibly stern and spoke to me in black and white terms, I knew it

5

was his Wood element making him seem angrier than he actually felt. And, when my aunt always seemed to be upset that I didn't visit her more, I realized that it was her Earth needing to serve and make me happy, not just a relative guilt-tripping me. In fact, conflicts and differences are rarely personal. More often they are brought on by elements being out of balance.

The Five Elements have filled a gap for me, a gap that for many people is filled with unnecessary guilt, shame, fear, frustration, and sadness. I've watched friends and acquaintances struggle and suffer because they don't have this easy and helpful system to help them understand, through the challenging times, themselves and others, or to let them really embrace the good times and good connections. As a person who spent most of my life in show business in performances around the world, the Five Elements also helped guide me through hectic schedules, unknown cultures, intense criticism, and the extreme competition of working on stage and in film and television.

I'm deeply grateful for my mom's early teachings. Instead of letting my true elements be destroyed by school or home life, she taught me to embrace them and to be proud of my elemental makeup. And she was right: Through countless personal, social, and business relationships in my life, the Five Elements have never failed me. Rather, this system has helped me to excel in most everything I ever attempted—and to be OK when I didn't. It has "saved" my life more than once. Ultimately, it helps all—without exception—to foster a truer and deeper acceptance of themselves and others than they could possibly muster on their own.

An Ancient System from China

The system of the Five Elements began with acupuncture, a healing practice that grew out of a four- to five-thousand-year-old Asian medical tradition. In *The Inner Canon*, a two-thousand-year-old medical text, Chinese physicians and scholars theorized that the universe is composed of forces represented by Water, Wood, Fire, Earth, and Metal—the Five Elements. They proposed that human behavior, emotions, and health are influenced by these elements and that people's personalities can be distinguished by them.

One of the reasons that this system is hard for us to comprehend in the West is because the innate energy, intuition, and personal rhythm that we are born with is often destroyed by family, school, and society.

Professor J. R. Worsley (1923–2003) is credited with bringing Five Element acupuncture to the West. After receiving his doctorate in acupuncture in Asia in the fifties, he founded the College of Traditional Chinese Acupuncture in England in 1956 and, by 1975, also had a location in the United States. Worsley taught that every human being is born with an imbalance in the Five Elements and that that imbalance is the underlying cause of illness. If you can find the imbalance, you can cure the illness and prevent other illnesses. He also taught that imbalances in the five elements could influence more than just physical health—they had an impact on the extent to which one grows socially and emotionally to become more self-aware and, ultimately, happier. He was clear that he was passing along a system that was practiced for thousands of years in China and was based on laws that do not change and will not change. He also warned that we are more complex than just five types and that it's important not to draw conclusions based on categorizations. Judgments and labels based on categorizations lead to faulty conclusions.

Worsley taught that ultimately it was possible to recognize the authentic self through an understanding of the Five Elements. Understanding this system and how your elemental combination affects your life can bring enlightenment and freedom because it can lift you out of judgment. He wanted his students to love one another and think beyond separateness to the true heart and soul of the person.

Why Haven't I Heard of the Five Elements?

Chances are you have heard of acupuncture, an ancient Chinese system for bringing the body back into balance by using hair-thin needles on different parts of the skin to activate certain acupressure points. You might also have heard of feng shui, a method for balancing the energies in rooms and spaces so that it can flow freely and assure health and good fortune for the people in that space. Embedded in these systems is the theory of the Five Elements: both acupuncture and feng shui draw almost exclusively on its wisdom.

However, you may not have heard much about the Five Elements themselves. We can trace this back to Chairman Mao Zedong, the Chinese dictator who dominated China for much of the twentieth century. He came into power in 1949 and by the 1960s he had suppressed the Five Elements and feng shui, as well as many other cultural and spiritual practices in China—anything that would promote individuality. He then created "traditional Chinese medicine" (TCM), which is not actually a historical method but a grouping of unrelated and sometimes competing modalities, so he could have one unified medicine. In his quest to "modernize" China, he attempted to erase the past because such ancient systems as the Five Elements—a system that recognized people as individuals and helped them to lead happier and healthier lives—threatened his agenda. He sought to make everyone think the same, feel the same, look the same, and be the same so he could completely control them. Mao's desire for ultimate power over his people seems to be the reason why he collapsed the vast country's five time zones into one (which is a huge problem today), all because he wanted people to eat their rice at the same time.

It is said that Chairman Mao deeply understood that feng shui has the power to make people wealthy and powerful. He worried that someone might use it to produce an emperor to take his throne. Therefore he burned and destroyed many documents, buildings, and artifacts that recorded the ancient wisdom of the Five Elements and feng shui. Much of the tradition's history is gone forever.

The Five Elements Expand Your Compassion

Even so, thanks to the work of people like Professor J. R. Worsley, and the brave people of China, knowledge of the Five Elements survived the reign of Mao. The system is uncomplicated, straightforward, and deeply enlightening, helping us to stay in balance physically, spiritually, emotionally, and mentally—or to return to balance after unhealthy living, illness, stress, or other disturbances. Once you know the tendencies of Water, Wood, Fire, Earth, and Metal, you also start to understand the pulse of certain eras, the architecture and

9

emotional feel of buildings, the culture and heritage of countries, the demeanor and personalities of animals, and even the political climates and attitudes of certain parts of the world.

At first, you may feel that the elements put people (or situations) into categories or boxes, or stick shallow and arbitrary labels on them. In my experience however, when you start working with this system, it forces you to reexamine and expand what you think you know about people and events. It squashes our generalizations and our assumptions, reminding us that everyone and everything is an individual and everyone has a different rhythm. For example, it's easy for a Water, who spends a lot of time ruminating and thinking about life, to get depressed or feel overwhelmed under stress. A Wood's likely response to stress, on the other hand, is to become angry and aggressive with people. A Fire will need lively, energetic people with fun activities to keep him or her in balance. An Earth will want supportive friends and family around to help out. And a Metal will probably detach from people and things while under stress.

Once you understand that *everyone* has a challenge with his or her dominant element, and reacts to stress in their own way, then you no longer feel alone in your experiences. The elements remind us that we are all human, we are all flawed, and most of us have a buckling point when we're stressed. The elements will help you forgive yourself and others when that buckling point comes. An awareness of them will ease your tendency toward judgment and allow you to feel true admiration and appreciation of yourself and all human beings.

I believe that the Five Elements can enable us to think beyond separateness. This is something I deeply appreciate about them. While we don't all have to be friends, we can have a true understanding of one another, knowing that we are all connected through human experience. Knowing this makes life and relationships less stressful. It naturally takes us beyond the influence of our genes and our upbringing. It's like having a life raft that will help you to stay afloat and not crash into the rocks. You can also offer your life raft to others to prevent needless pain and suffering for them, as well.

What to Expect from This Book

The personality tests developed by Katharine Cook Briggs and Isabel Briggs Myers have helped businesses everywhere build teamwork among their employees, not to mention helping people find their true vocation in life and true love on dating sites. The enneagram (nine type) system popularized by Oscar Ichazo and Claudio Naranjo, based on work by G. I. Gurdjieff and ancient authors, has provided a useful model for understanding human personalities. Likewise, the Five Elements will empower you to understand yourself and engage with others in a way that is immediate, practical, potent, and lasting. It will create a new understanding of all relationships and cultivate a happier you.

This book is for you if you have ever thought to yourself:

- ○ "I can't believe she said that!"
- ○ "In a thousand years, I wouldn't have done what he did!"
- ○ "That's *so* unbelievable!"

11

Or if you have:

- ○ Wondered why people do what they do
- ○ Been confused about why people say what they say
- ○ Wanted to cry, scream, or laugh hysterically because of how people act
- ○ Been confused about why your partner never changes or your brother, mother, or sister behave the same dysfunctional way again and again
- ○ Not known how to talk to someone because they are so different from you
- ○ Been shocked speechless by the way someone has treated you
- ○ Been interested in feeling less misunderstood, angry, or alone
- ○ Been interested in having more ease and more of a sense of humor in life

The Five Elements can help you figure out people and situations so that you aren't perplexed by them anymore. The concept will help you be able to talk to people, understand events, have true compassion, and go through life without taking everything so painfully to heart. It gives you a key to being able to accept and let go, rather than be in judgment and hold on. It invites you to be authentic, to connect with others in a way that you may not have experienced before, and to let go of limiting beliefs.

As you learn, you'll be able to sit back, breathe, and understand that all people have their own limitations (especially under stress), even when they are trying their very best. You'll be able to connect with others and break through

12

energy barriers that are there even when our eyes cannot see them. This system will bring you peace, joy, and an understanding that can help you everywhere with everyone—in your workplace, at home, and in your social life. It's a proven way to make your life easier and less challenging.

In fact, understanding the Five Elements will help you become your best self.

NIKE ▶ **Just Do It.**

●	**WATER**	Let's have dinner while we talk about doing it.
	WOOD	It's done. I did it yesterday.
	FIRE	Woo-hoo! Everyone's doing it!
	EARTH	Can we do it together?
	METAL	It's not about doing; it's about being.

CHAPTER ONE

The Water Personality
Searching for Meaning

■

Is there no way out of the mind?
—SYLVIA PLATH, POET

WATER ARCHETYPES:
   The Philosopher ► The Thinker ► The Baby ► The Prince/Princess

THE SEASON:
   Winter (hibernation)

STRESS RESPONSE:
   Internalize and isolate

FAMOUS PEOPLE WITH WATER ELEMENT:
   Kurt Cobain
   Stevie Nicks
   Janis Joplin
   Nicholas Cage
   Kevin Costner

KURT COBAIN

IF WATER PEOPLE WERE ANIMALS:
   The Turtle
   (wise and with its own, slow rhythm)

The cafés in Paris, the hookah lounges in the Middle East, and the urban coffeehouses in America are filled with them. They love to sit with close friends, ruminating about life, waxing eloquent about all that is right and wrong with the world. They are great conversationalists, and the deeper the conversations, the better.

Waters are poignant in their conversations. The philosopher type of Water (we'll get into the two types of Waters later) doesn't want to waste time talking about silly stuff or watching things on TV that don't seem to have much meaning. Most of them would rather not talk at all than make small talk. But share something meaningful, sincere, and earnest with a Water, and he or she will be all ears. Let her dive deep into your words so she can discover something new, and you will have a friend for life.

Water people love to plumb the depths of life. They lose themselves blissfully in the arts, with a childlike playfulness, becoming hypnotized by complex musical scores. Waters are the people at gallery openings who stand in front of one painting for hours, talking about its lines, its colors, its use of angles and curves. They are the ones who walk slowly through the rain, soaking up the fresh smell of the wet pavement and listening to the droplets splashing on the ground. Grocery store aisles are strewn with them standing, staring and pondering the fifty different types of bread that line the shelves. Waters everywhere are taking their time. The word *hurry* is not in their vocabulary, and this calm plays out in the way they speak, walk, act, react, and live. Theirs is a slower rhythm.

Many Waters look a little messy. They often flourish in clutter. Waters' clothes might be wrinkled, their shirttails half out. Comfort is everything, which for men might mean shorts with a pair of ugly tennis shoes and black pull-up socks, while the women wear nondescript clothing that doesn't neces-

16

sarily match. A blue polyester parka with gray sweatpants and purple UGGs works just fine for Waters. The hair? Probably in a knot on top of their head, whether they are male or female. If it's not in a knot, it's straight down and unkempt. Fancy haircuts and fashion just aren't on their list of priorities—there are much bigger things to think about in life.

Waters want to build lives fully aligned with their personal values and all that they deem important in life. The gifts that these Waters bring to our rushed world are the ability to slow down, have patience, and not miss the details. Waters have mastery in their heads, and if we are lucky enough, they will record it in a book, in a song, or on the big screen.

The most creative and artistic people have strong Water, and art produced by them is the most awe-inspiring. They are alluring and wise poets and writers, hypnotizing and dynamic dancers and painters. Music like ethnic folk songs and the blues; poetry like that of Rumi, Hafiz, and Anaïs Nin; lyrics like those of Joan Baez and Judy Collins—these are all Water element.

Water musicians like Bob Marley and the former Cat Stevens (now Yusuf Islam) have changed the world with their lyrics. Ernest Hemingway wrote influential American novels. Beatrix Potter, beloved for her children's books, was also a conservationist who helped to preserve the Lake District in England for future generations. Jean Houston, a visionary thinker and philosopher of our time, is inspiring people with her spoken and written words, as did the late Wayne Dyer with his sage quotes and timeless books. These are just a few of the people with strong Water who keep our world meaningful, sincere, and significant.

Waters find poignancy in meaningful rituals, symbols, and traditions. Japan is strong in its Water element (and also Metal). The Japanese take everyday

17

tasks and make them refined, thoughtful, and beautiful. Store clerks, cleaners, cooks, office workers, gas station attendants, and others treat their work as art. The Japanese people have many rituals—greeting rituals, water rituals, food and drink rituals, rituals for the different seasons, and even suicide rituals. These rituals are woven with mythology, metaphor, and stories and bring meaning to their lives. They are deeply philosophical and profound. The movie *Departures*, which took the Academy Award for Best Foreign Film in 2008, shows the power of the death ritual in Japan. Steps are taken to wash the body of the deceased, the body is ritually dressed and made up, and several relevant items are placed in the coffin for the deceased to take into the afterlife. The head of the body is placed to the north or west, which reflects the orientation of Western Buddhism. The ritual is done with creativity, beauty, significance, and meaning—very much in the Water mode.

Waters use ritual, as well as symbolism, to make sense of life's events. If Waters cannot make sense of life, it can look very warped to them. They tend to live deep within themselves, where they can feel secluded and alone. Imagine diving into a swimming pool, then opening your eyes under water and looking up. You can see the edges of the pool and even the people and activities going on up above the water, but everything is distorted—the people are out of proportion and their voices are muffled. This is how life can look and sound to Waters when they go deep within. With their unending thoughts, they can be prone to depression. When they are depressed, everything can become exaggerated and look very different from what others see, hear, and feel. They start to believe that they aren't worth anyone's time. Remember that children's song "Nobody likes me, everybody hates me—I think I'll eat some worms"? This is the reality of an imbalanced Water. I am a secondary Water and if I am imbalanced because of stress or difficulties in my life, I go on Facebook and I can get very despondent. I see things like "33 Animals Who Are Extremely Disappointed in You," and I believe the article was written just for me—I don't get the humor. As I sit staring at the wall thinking, "What's the point of it all," I remember the dangers of being a Water and I call a Fire friend, who tells me that the article is a joke. Phew! I decide that, when depressed, Waters aren't well suited to watch the news or even their News Feed on Facebook. Though the news can give us a bigger picture of the world around us and what is happening in other countries, it can send a Water into a pit of doom. The world is just too much at times! The headline of Syrian children washing up on beaches in Turkey will naturally throw anyone into sadness and hopelessness. But Waters can also get depressed if they read that "50,000 People Are Hugging Right Now," because each Water feels like the only one in the world who isn't getting a hug right now. Buck up, Waters! People love hugging you, and you are some of the deepest and most penetrating, imaginative, and intelligent minds there are.

Waters Live in Their Minds

Taking a trip to Paris with my boyfriend, Brian, was as good as life could get. We strolled the tree-lined streets, enjoying quaint French cafés and the un-hurried pace of the waiters. Brian noticed every detail about the city. He sipped his red wine slowly and spoke poetically about the undertones of the grapes. As sounds from street musicians caught his ear, he would describe the differences between the accordion and the violin. He waxed romantic

19

about philosophy, politics, and the state of the world, adding his own brilliant ideas to the mix. You had to be well-read to keep up with Brian, and I welcomed the challenge. His stories were full of wit and sociopolitical references.

But everything went very slowly with Brian. The energy of Paris was light and joyful, but the energy of Brian was often slow and heavy. Brian had no urgency to get anywhere, and he was usually late. After hours of sitting in sidewalk restaurants planning the future, he would get overwhelmed and forlorn, with the weight of what seemed like the whole world on his shoulders. He often felt depressed. Low energy was one of his vulnerabilities.

When he went to a negative place, Brian's depression would turn to fear and paranoia. Then he would speak of his friends as if their successes were somehow against him. He always noticed what his friends and family hadn't done for him (instead of what they *had* done for him). Just the thought or sight of them when he was in this state was enough to trigger these thoughts in him. He was resentful of others who had more money, more fame, or more public acknowledgment. When Brian sank deep into his Water, his view of the world could be incredibly unreal. He needed a Fire to pull him out. Unfortunately, I am primarily a Wood, efficient and driven, so Brian's depression mystified me and felt narcissistic. As much as I wanted to, I wasn't able to offer much help.

Waters work in mysterious ways, and for most people, they are the most difficult of the Five Elements personalities to grasp. One reason for the confusion is that there are two distinctly different types of Water people. Sometimes a person is just one type of Water, and sometimes they are both.

20

The First Type of Water

The first type of Water person has the archetype of the philosopher. This Water is the deep thinker described on the previous pages, someone who ponders and seeks out meaning in every part of life. She spends time in her mind and often loves reading, writing, journaling, and thinking but isn't drawn to big groups or crowds of people.

This type of Water is usually interested in the past, from personal histories to the histories of countries and events. Preservationists are usually Water—they make sense of the present by understanding the past.

When they meet a new person, these Waters are eager to discover information about this person's birthplace, home, and childhood. Both home and meaningful journeys away from home are important for them. They are like the loggerhead turtles that hatch on beaches around the world. Shortly after birth, they take to the ocean to begin an epic migration, sometimes traveling thousands of miles. Then, often decades later, the turtles return to the beach where they were born so they can mate and lay their own eggs. Female loggerhead turtles sense the magnetic field of the coastline and use it to find their way home. Like the magnetic draw of home for a turtle, there is a magnetic draw of home for a Water person.

This Harley-Riding Hippie Is a Water Type

Peter Fonda stood surrounded by young, beautiful twenty-first-century college kids who had been invited to his birthday party at a historic mansion in Rancho Santa Fe, California. They were members of an acting class from the

University of California at San Diego. The celebration was for him but also for the students, who had been studying his films for several months.

I had been hired to belly dance for him for the second year in a row. Both times, I wondered if the throngs of college kids truly understood Peter Fonda's place in one of Hollywood's most elite acting dynasties, joining his father, Henry, and his sister, Jane, to become a film icon in the sixties—forty years earlier.

A wealthy philanthropist hosted Peter Fonda's birthday parties, and they were always hopping with loud, upbeat music and graced by a giant birthday cake with a huge red-white-and-blue motorcycle made of frosting on top of it. The actor had become inextricably connected to "Captain America," the name of the chopper he rode in the movie *Easy Rider*, considered the most famous motorcycle in the world. The conversations were upbeat, the alcohol kept flowing, and platters of food continuously emerged from the kitchen. The energy soared high, but Peter stayed even-keeled, even mellow.

The first year I danced for Peter, I summed up his elements right away. He was a Water with Metal, and his Water was very interesting for me to observe. He spoke softly and eloquently to student after student about acting, directing, performing, humanity, and digging deep within for self-discovery. Any student who wanted to speak with him could, but it was a very one-on-one endeavor. He wasn't speaking to the masses, he wasn't laughing with groups of people, and he wasn't flitting from room to room. Peter held the space of the party, owning a corner and allowing people to come to him. He stood almost still and rather quiet, containing his energy—not rigidly but fluidly. He engaged each person as if he or she were the only one in the room and there were nothing else to grab his attention.

I listened intently to his conversations, which expressed insight about the

22

world, enlightened wisdom about the arts and spirituality, and a poetic philosophy about connection to people and our vulnerability as human beings. After each person spoke with him, he emitted a sense of oneness, and subsequently I could sense an enthusiasm from the partygoers that we were all in this together. The actor had gracefully connected the dots for these young people, helping them to feel significant.

Then came my time to perform. Outside, under the stars, with twinkle lights laced through the trees and peacocks roaming the tiered acreage and gardens, I danced.

Peter sat in a chair center stage and took in every move. He watched my hands and my feet, and nodded intently when I did a certain gesture or turned a specific way. He seemed intrigued by the dance and followed up with curious conversation after the performance.

He compared the dance to other forms of physical movement and remarked about the spiritual nature of it. He used the words *intuition, heart,* and *feeling* when speaking about the dance. And as a typical Water would, he embraced creativity, reflection, and eccentricity, while promoting individuality and freedom. He spoke about the divine feminine and women as the essence of life. He was easygoing and powerful at the same time—a concentrated and yet fluid force of kindness and intensity.

The Second Type of Water

The second type of Water person has the archetype of the new baby in its wonderment and playfulness. She enjoys cuddling, giggling, and being coddled.

She is the adult who hasn't lost her childlike eagerness and glow. There is often a sweet naiveté in this type of Water person. She might follow the crowd or befriend a stranger—as a toddler does—because it is fun and interesting. Curiosity is a part of the Water "baby," and it makes these people very endearing, spontaneous, and lighthearted.

However, doing things themselves and following through with ideas are not strong suits for this second type of Water. They expect others to take care of them as they journey along, and this can lead to selfishness and narcissism. They may act like little princes or princesses, requiring convenience and expecting to be served. After all, the world revolves around a baby.

The ideas of the Water "baby" can be unique and inspiring—even brilliant—and usually stand out in any business or organization. Catchy jingles—such as "Oh, I wish I were an Oscar Mayer wiener," "I am stuck on Band-Aid 'cause Band-Aid's stuck on me," "Like a good neighbor, State Farm is there," and "Plop, plop, fizz, fizz—Oh what a relief it is"—were probably all thought of by Waters.

But the challenge lies in following through. Putting ideas into action is quite difficult for this type of Water, who often lacks the motivation and commitment to carry their brilliance to fruition (they need a Wood to push them along). They can get lost in life and overwhelmed by the details of having so many ideas that they do nothing. As the manager or boss of a Water, you will do well to tap into their creativity, but don't hold their feet to the fire to complete the project; find someone else in the company to get it done. This is a great strategy because Waters yearn for someone else to manage the details for them, and you will get a better result in the end.

Even though the two types of Water—the playful baby and the wise philosopher—are distinctly different, both usually have a yin energy. The yin (inner

24

focus) makes their playfulness softer than the playfulness of a Fire, for example, which is big, bold, and far-reaching (yang). In relationships, Waters tend to be quieter, more introverted, and more private than other elements. This makes for an interesting mix when they are partnered with people who are in the limelight.

While balanced Waters can be completely captivating, imbalanced Waters in the public eye can ironically have both low self-esteem and huge egos. Performers may have hundreds, thousands, or millions of fans, but those throngs of people may not really love *them* and could even stop admiring them after the curtain closes. This can lead their big egos to crash so painfully that they get depressed. The good news is that if they are balanced Waters, they take it all in stride.

Many musicians, singers, and songwriters have a strong Water element. Words have great meaning for Waters, as does sound, pitch, vibration, and musical scores. Music can also be a type of ritual as musicians get lost in the composition of songs. With rhythm and tones they travel to another place, and music acts as a healing modality to bring them out of sadness, depression, and melancholy. It can be very therapeutic to experience words through song.

Dwight Yoakam—a Visionary Water

Dwight Yoakam is a musician, actor, film director, entrepreneur, and pioneer in modern country music. He is a Renaissance man who is called "too unique for Nashville and too authentic for Hollywood." As *Vanity Fair* declared, "Yoakam strides the divide between rock's lust and country's lament."

25

In 2005, I had come off a year of performing around the world as a Marilyn Monroe impersonator. I had done more than two hundred shows. But I wasn't just any Monroe look-alike; I was Marilyn Monroe if she'd been a belly dancer. My act was comic, quirky, and unique.

After my long run, I was really tired of Marilyn and was happy that I had upcoming contracts for regular Middle Eastern dance performances in India and Africa. But then I received an e-mail from Dwight Yoakam's assistant asking if I would like to meet with him in Los Angeles to talk about collaborating on a show with my Marilyn Monroe act. Dwight Yoakam? Wasn't he a cowboy? Or an actor? Or did I hear somewhere that he had twenty-one Grammy nominations? I looked him up on the Internet and couldn't imagine this honky-tonk star being interested in my show. I asked my smattering of cowgirl friends from Texas to Montana if they had heard of him. They asked me if I was nuts. Of course, they'd heard of this legend in country music. But they couldn't understand why he would be interested in a belly dancer. I was intrigued too.

Before our meeting, I had every negative stereotype in my head of a male country music star. I expected Dwight to be antisocial, physically awkward, and only semi-intelligent. I wasn't sure what he had planned for my act, and I wondered if I was about to be the butt of a cruel joke. Would he set me up for mockery? I wasn't sure, but I did know that I would have to explain belly dancing to him and probably the motive behind my impersonation of Marilyn. I was preparing myself to educate him on a lot of levels, and I wasn't looking forward to trying to get him to get it. This was a game I had played many times.

I walked into Dwight's office atop a high-rise in Los Angeles, and not only was he a complete gentleman, but he also inquired meaningfully about my act, how I created it, where my instincts as a performer came from, and why I thought

Marilyn should have been a belly dancer. He came out from behind the desk and we sat together on comfy overstuffed chairs while we talked. He discussed the art of belly dance and nailed every aspect about the history of the dance, how it grew from folklore to cabaret, and the misconceptions of it in America. He talked about dance in myth and religion, referring to Greek goddesses like Terpsichore and the evolution of dance from ancient times. He spoke softly but powerfully, as if he were a university professor teaching a course about the arts, feminism, and the impact of empowered women in a dance form that the West misunderstands and debases. We talked in depth about my Marilyn act. He thought it was brilliant. He had acquired one of my DVDs and told me how much he appreciated my comedic timing and the difficulty of what I pulled off.

Dwight Yoakam spoke eloquently and with a great deal of respect for my work. I found him to be curious, clever, and beyond bright. He conversed with me in a sophisticated manner with meaning behind every word, and he listened with rapt interest and complete attention. Between his sentences, it was as if I could see his thought process—his mind was full of new ideas every second. He was Water at its very best.

Weeks later, I drove to Hollywood to open for Dwight at the House of Blues to a sold-out crowd. As I got ready backstage with two other performers, who were a part of the warm-up show, I noticed January Jones, Vince Vaughn, Salma Hayek, Josh Groban, and others milling around the dressing rooms and backstage areas. The place was full of celebrities because they all adored Dwight.

Dwight Yoakam is a Water/Metal and is bubbling over with all of the best traits of a Water. He calls himself a hillbilly, but if that's true, then the connotation of *hillbilly* has to change.

27

Waters Get Stuck

Tom liked grocery shopping. It gave him time to get away from the stress of family life and to be in his own world. Working a full-time job, taking care of his aging parents, and being a good father to his son and a supportive partner to his wife wasn't always easy. The grocery store was a place where he could chill out. He slowly roamed the aisles looking for the best buys. New products caught his eye. When he reached his favorite food aisles, he often got stuck there. He could spend more than an hour in the meat section after telling his wife he would be home in thirty minutes.

Time was not on Tom's radar; the half-price ten-pound ham was. Tom compared the ham with the other meats, the prices, where the farms were located, where the meat was shipped from, and the quality of the beef. He would request to speak to the butcher about the bacon, hot dogs, steak, and sausages. Many of the meats were half price because the expiration date was looming. It was not a concern for Tom. He knew that meat could be eaten several days after the expiration date, and anyway, he could add the new meat to his already full freezer of previously purchased meat.

Tom often got stuck in the cereal aisle as well. There was so much to choose from: Raisin Bran? Frosted Mini-Wheats? Life? Special K? Special K Protein? Special K Gluten Free? Special K Red Berries? It was dizzying. He had coupons for everything and sorting through them took up even more time. Tom didn't *collect* coupons; he would think of them when walking out of the house to do the shopping. Only then would he return to his computer and start the process of finding the best coupons for his meaningful quest.

When Tom's wife told him that she wanted to consume less sugar and carbohydrates while eating gluten-free, free-range, and organic food, her choice made Tom's life even trickier. He now had to spend more time finding coupons for the expensive health foods and more time staring at the ingredients and reading the lists of possible allergens, preservatives, toxins, and sugars. Tom secretly felt liberated by all of it.

Water types need their own space and need to feel safe, whether they're out and about or at home. Their personal space may be messy (it usually is) and filled with old blankets, pillows, chairs, and random stuff, but it's a comfortable place for them to think and discover—even if it's the grocery store.

Waters Need Time Alone—Without Getting Lost Inside Their Heads

Waters are very good at being alone. As a Water child grows, she learns that being alone can be very liberating. In fact, Waters need to withdraw and surrender to some darkness, but they also need to watch that they don't become socially isolated or trapped in their own inner turmoil. For Waters, maintaining a link to humanity prevents them from becoming despondent.

Tom's love of grocery shopping was harmless. It gave him the space to go deep in himself and refresh. But in general, to be good partners and effective workers, Waters need to remind themselves what motivates them and keeps them from retreating to their own world of thoughts, obsessions, and even negativity. If they retreat too far, they become paranoid. They will miss appointments, fail to prioritize timelines and people, and mañana—tomorrow—

29

will become the mantra. But, as we know, mañana never comes, and Waters can fall into the murky lake of procrastination.

The procrastination and tardiness of a Water person can drive other people bonkers, especially if the Water is highly intelligent. It baffles others how intelligent Waters can seem so oblivious of time passing. It is good to know that the Water personality factors into this predicament. It helps others to release the judgment and stop taking the tardiness personally.

So if you are a Water (see the quiz at the end of this chapter), ask yourself: What motivates me to stay positive and keep going forward? Exercise? A group of friends? An outdoor activity? Theater? Music?

If, as a Water, you cannot think of something to keep your mind on task, befriend a Wood. You will get coached, inspired, and motivated to get the task done and not get distracted or lose energy for the job at hand. Or befriend a Fire. Woods will honor time and a Fire will cheerlead you to complete that project, get that book written, or finish that painting. Coming from a Water, that project, book, or painting will probably be a masterpiece.

As Diana Nyad, one of the greatest long-distance swimmers in history, said after she swam from Cuba to Florida over one of the most dangerous straits of water in the world at age sixty-four, "Summon your spirit for something that moves you and don't fear failure," and "Make this the prime of your life, whatever age you are, whatever life circumstances you find yourself [in], and never believe in imposed limitations." While she is primarily a Wood, this advice works especially well for Waters because Waters can get stuck in fear and limitations, which prevent them from meeting their goals and fulfilling their desires. Their path of growth is to trust the people around them and not let their own thoughts dictate their daily existence.

30

DO!

- Do take time out every day to move and stretch, preferably out-doors or with others.

  Waters tend to seclude themselves physically and emotionally. Moving and stretching will help to keep you from isolating and withdrawing from people and the world.

DON'T!

- Don't always believe your worst fears and paranoia.

  If you are a Water, you will have a hard time trusting that people are good and on your side. Tap into faith with the help of good friends, positive affirmations, and involvement with positive people.

The Waters' Natural Rhythm—Creativity and Flow

I was miserable in school. In eighth grade, students teased me mercilessly, and teachers sent me to the principal's office for my green hair, checkered Vans, or whatever else they felt was disturbing the other kids. Ashland, Oregon, in 1981 was conservative—at least at the junior high school—and not at all the funky hotbed of artists and healers it is today. I wanted out, and my mom listened. She came up with several options, including homeschooling with a wise and insightful woman named Catherine, who was a Water.

Once I crossed the threshold into Catherine's little house, she allowed me to create my own path, literally and figuratively, through her home. She served me a small lunch and always remarked on the colors of the carrots, the plumpness of the raisins, and how they commingled in the tiny glass bowl. Then she invited me to write anything that came to my mind, in poetry, prose, doodles—it didn't matter. The important part was to let it flow. As I followed her instructions, Catherine sat at the piano playing Mozart, Beethoven, Brahms, Bach, Chopin—and it all flowed masterfully from her fingers. I don't remember what I wrote, but it was likely about not fitting in, being teased, feeling alone and misunderstood by other kids. I probably cried.

What I remember now—and what has stayed with me my whole life—is that Catherine allowed me to go wherever my heart and mind took me, but she didn't allow me to wallow in depression or tears. She helped me tap into my creative side and flow with it. In her care, I felt free. I also felt empowered, which was remarkable for a twelve-year-old girl who had been ostracized and ridiculed almost daily. Because Catherine trusted me to write without rules, without time limits—simply with the backdrop of beautiful music—I came to love and trust my own solitary existence. She gave me access to my creativity and my solitude. Within a short time, pressured by my father and wanting to have friends in my life, I went back to school. But thanks to a Water, I never disliked being alone again, and I fell in love with me.

32

Waters and Emotion: Fear

Every element is governed by different organs and by different emotions. It can be difficult for Westerners to understand that the strengths, weaknesses, and qualities of physical organs can affect emotional experiences and well-being, but this idea is very much alive in the East. In fact, traditional Chinese medicine (TCM) is based on this awareness. For a Water type, those organs are the kidneys and bladder, and the emotion associated with them is fear.

Water is the first of the Five Elements, which are represented by a wheel (see page 244). When you work with the wheel, you start with Water. It is the beginning—the newborn baby. Nothing comes before it. This may be why some Waters feel parentless, alone, and without support in this life. There also may be a pull to the past—even past lifetimes. Many people who believe that life does not end completely at death often also believe in being bonded to ancestors who have long passed on. Chinese medicine says that this ancestral knowledge is stored in the kidneys, and it expresses itself through Water types who subconsciously remember the dangers of life—because they know they have been through it before.

Learn to Transcend the Fear

When I was about fourteen, my friend Kirstin and I often walked downtown together in Ashland, Oregon. We would pass the Victorian home with the red-headed hippie guy, the modern apartment where our English teacher lived, and the craftsman with the big reflective window so we could fix our hair and makeup. Then there was that dog. That dog who always barked ferociously and bared its teeth. As we approached, the dog would run along the chain-link fence, threatening to jump over. I was afraid he would tear our limbs off. Every time we walked by, I would freeze and want to turn back.

One day Kirstin said to me, "You know that dogs can sense fear, right?" I had no idea what she was talking about. Kirstin told me that when people are scared, they produce pheromones that dogs can smell, even from far away, and dogs react to it in violent ways. She told me to test it out.

The next time I walked down East Main Street, I decided I wasn't scared. I completely blocked out any fear. I focused on my purpose of walking downtown, and I walked right by that dog. I couldn't just pretend that I wasn't scared. If I put on a good face but still sweated, the dog would pick up on my scared smell. But I was resolute. I turned off my fear. And it worked. As I walked by . . . nothing happened. Not even a whimper. The dog didn't bark or run along the fence in rabid salivation.

Whether Waters are scared of something tangible, like that dog, or intangible, like the fear of success or failure, they need to find a way to switch gears so that they don't get stuck. Even though Water is my secondary element, I still need to work with it, and conquering my fear was an important lesson. It helped me decide which thoughts were useful and which weren't, so I could become a healthier person.

My friend William never travels because he has convinced himself that the world is a scary place. There are thieves, terrorists, rapists, murderers, and con men all over the world—not to mention severe weather patterns and airplanes that crash! So instead of taking a risk and enjoying different countries, cities, people, and cultures, he stays home. Yet every time I drag William along on a trip, he loves it and swears he will keep traveling. Once home again, the fear comes back. Waters often allow fear to make decisions for them. When this happens, their lives become less fully lived than they otherwise might have been.

To move through fear is often difficult, but for Waters who can do this, it is a great gift for their lives and the lives of others. Otherwise, there is a risk of missing out on real experiences, connections, and intimacy with people.

If a Water person in your life is fearful of stepping forward as her best self, you can help her by simplifying the steps she needs to take and reminding her when she forgets. Helping her identify and address what scares her from moving forward is a step in the right direction. After that, baby steps are best. Helping her break down the process of moving forward into manageable pieces and then being there for her during the journey will help her realize that, for the most part, daily life is not as daunting as her imagination tells her it is.

A Top Doctor Finds His Rhythm—and Leaves His Fortune Behind

Pacific Beach in San Diego, California, is home to skateboarders, beer drinkers, bikini beauties, pot smokers, volleyball players, runners, joggers, bicycle riders, tourists, locals, surfers, bird-watchers, beach lovers, and lots of partiers. It's a cacophony of amped up, sunshiny people soaking up the best of California. Then there is Slomo, the guy who Rollerblades in slow motion along the boardwalk. He moves in complete contrast to the busy energy of beach life around him. He's there every day, and if you visit the boardwalk, you will undoubtedly encounter him.

Slomo, a Water, wasn't always Slomo. He was Dr. John Kitchin, a successful and wealthy MD with a degree in neurology and in psychology. He lived in a mansion, owned an exotic pet farm, and drove a BMW and a Ferrari. But after a health scare, he gave it all up. He decided to Rollerblade right out of the stress of the medical world and into his authentic rhythm of Water. He is now in his seventies, and every single day he Rollerblades up and down the boardwalk in slow motion while acrobatically balancing on one skate and then the other. When first laying eyes on Slomo, people shake their heads because what he does is so unreal, skating in slow motion through all the hustle and bustle. It takes time to adjust to his rhythm as he rolls by at a pace that is slower than most people walking.

When Slomo was still Dr. Kitchin, he asked himself, "How much of today promoted me spiritually, and how much of today promoted me financially?" As a typical Water, it bothered him that his life was losing its deeper meaning because of his career in the fast-paced world of a top doctor. Then, in a drastic move, which he made despite fear of the consequences, he gave it all up for a slower pace, a simpler lifestyle, and a slower day-to-day existence. And just like the water that gently but powerfully rises and falls on the shores of the San Diego beaches, Slomo ebbs and flows up and down the coast for miles without regard to time, in his own slow rhythm, honoring his journey.

Robert De Niro—a Talented, Heart-Centered Water

In 1990, I was a struggling actress in Fort Lauderdale, Florida. I booked a job as an extra on the set of the movie *Cape Fear*, with Robert De Niro, Jessica Lange, Nick Nolte, and Juliette Lewis.

Although I was new to South Florida, I had done a lot of extra work in Los Angeles, and I was used to the drill. I would wait in a hot room overstuffed with two hundred other struggling actors, all desperate to get discovered. At some point, the director of the movie would walk through the room and pick people for his background. I had been through this with Oliver Stone on the set of *The Doors* and on TV shows, including *Dynasty*.

When I arrived on the set, I was told to go to the holding area and wait. I knew it could be hours. Or never. I found a corner, pulled out my crossword puzzle, and sank into the moist heat of the afternoon. When I was told that Martin Scorsese was coming through to pick his background, I didn't really care. I was getting paid for the day, I figured I wouldn't be chosen, and I was content sitting on the floor in a corner, doing puzzles and reading. Marty—as he's known—slowly walked through the sea of extras looking at each face in the crowd. He came around to my corner, our eyes met, and he chose me. He chose me! He needed two people out of the hundreds and he chose me?

I was escorted to the set. I walked with my head down and bumped into a man about my height, five feet four. I looked up and the man apologized for bumping into me. Holy crap—it was Robert De Niro. He was kind. Sweet, even! He asked if my head was OK. What? My head was splendid because it was talking to Robert De Niro.

For the next two days, I was treated as part of the team. I had the privilege to sit and watch two Water types—Robert De Niro (a Water/Wood) and Martin Scorsese (a Water/Fire) work at their art. I witnessed their conversations, their decisions, their brainstorming sessions. The relationship between them was a dance of mutual respect and admiration, very much a Water relationship. Together they found meaning in the script, explored the motives, reached

37

deep into the words, and transcended the story with some of the greatest acting and directing in the world.

The scene I was in was small. It consisted of a confrontation between Nick Nolte's and Robert De Niro's characters. Between takes Scorsese and De Niro spoke at length about the nook of the booth that De Niro would sit in, and how his character would lean onto the bar table. The two of them even discussed the best angle and pressure of how De Niro would pound his Bible on the table. Scorsese and De Niro huddled together in the corners, away from the rest of the crew, and delved deep into the way De Niro would move, the tone of voice he would use, and at which point he would deceptively smile . . . or not smile. This was, of course, after months of character preparation on his own. It was Method acting at its best—a theatrical practice that works well for Water types. It consists of dropping deep into the character and finding motivation for every move, action, behavior, and conversation. Method actors often go to extremes in preparing for their roles, in being able to find meaning and reason for what their character says and does. Method actors have been known to stay in character for weeks and months without speaking to family or friends as their real self. They will gain or lose large amounts of weight for the roles and undergo the same suffering their character experiences.

Nolte didn't resemble a Method actor, and if he was one, it didn't show. He also didn't resemble a Water and wasn't delving into the script or character while on the set. Instead he seemed to be a bit in a hurry, like he just wanted to get on with things; like a Wood might.

At one point during these magical forty-eight hours on set, Nick Nolte tried to engage De Niro in a conversation about football. De Niro couldn't even wrap his mind around it. I watched as De Niro delicately and kindly told Nolte that he wasn't really interested in football and was mostly watching coverage of the Gulf War. He said it with sensitivity and thoughtfulness and went back to his script—as most Waters would.

Waters and the Body

Most Water types are soft, with bodies that lack muscle tone, whether they are thin or heavy. Many Waters are slightly overweight or pudgy, with a round "butter face" and paunchy tummy. Some Waters (especially women) can seem quite delicate and precious. The Water walk is more of a swagger or a slow-paced stroll. They often stop for what seems like no reason, and they can hold up a moving crowd without realizing it.

Waters are governed by the kidneys and bladder, the organs that make up the urinary system. These organs need water to help flush waste from the blood. The kidneys filter the blood four hundred times a day! Waters need to drink plenty of—you guessed it—water to support their hard-working organs. People who do not drink enough water can easily develop bladder and kidney disorders due to the highly concentrated urine that they are passing.

The good news is that it is not difficult to support the kidneys and bladder. Drinking enough water is one way, and you can figure out how much you need by dividing your body weight, in pounds, in half. The number you get is the average amount of water you should drink in a day, in ounces. For instance, I hover around 133 pounds, so I need to drink about 67 ounces of water a day— more if I'm working out. You can also easily find water-intake formulas online to help calculate how much water you should be drinking.

39

In addition, drinking pomegranate juice will help prevent infections of the urinary tract, and consuming enough fiber helps to stave off constipation. Pomegranate juice and fibrous fruits and vegetables (or supplements) are available at most grocery stores. Constipation is not only uncomfortable, but also leads to other health problems, because the colon is close to the bladder and the pelvic floor muscles.

To live longer and more vibrantly, Waters need to avoid eating processed foods and drinking sodas, because they tax the bladder and kidneys. Keep in mind that it's not necessarily salt, sweets, breads, and fats that wreak havoc on the body—it's the processing of them.

For decades my mom has extolled the virtues of sea salt, and now it is finally coming to light that sea salt, with more than eighty minerals, may be one of the healthiest things you can put it in your mouth. Table salt, which is heavily processed, often contains only two minerals. Health coach Heather Dane recommends putting a flake of sea salt on your tongue or a bit of sea salt in your water to combat fatigue and dehydration. If nothing else, this may be a good time to switch from table salt to sea salt.

Avoiding processed foods, drinking more water, adding sea salt to your diet, and consuming Water-friendly foods and herbs will help support the bladder and kidneys. Unsupported or stressed Water organs may be vulnerable to infections, causing dark circles under the eyes, fatigue, edema, and brain fog.

YOUR KIDNEYS AND BLADDER LOVE THESE FOODS

(organic, please)

- Watermelon
- Apples
- Berries
- Unrefined olive oil
- Garlic
- Cauliflower

YOUR KIDNEYS AND BLADDER LOVE THESE HERBS

- Ginger root
- Juniper berry
- Parsley leaf
- Uva ursi
- Goldenseal root

Movement for Waters

Waters need to stretch, move, and shift their energies so that they don't get stuck. Start with gentle breathing and gentle movement. Also take thirty-minute walks three or four times a week. Walking helps with edema and fluid retention in the legs, which can be issues for Waters. Even taking baby steps toward staying balanced physically will help.

41

Waters usually do well at slow and fluid movement, as in Tai Chi and sports like surfing and swimming when noncompetitive and not in the style of "extreme" sports. The key for them is to keep moving, even if slowly; they don't need to work out at the gym to get their kidney and bladder energies pumping. Water types can do something as simple as walking to create healing and energy within their bodies.

Abraham Lincoln—a Watery President

Abraham Lincoln's decisions and actions as the sixteenth president of the United States still affect us more than 150 years later. He moved to abolish slavery, even at the cost of fighting a civil war; he worked to modernize the economy and the workings of government. Abe isn't around today to deal with the stressors of modern life in the twenty-first century, but even in his time, it was said that he battled insomnia, never took vacations, and had deep exhaustion. Who knows how this imbalance played out in his daily activities?

Abraham Lincoln was primarily a Water (with Metal). There are many signs that point to this. He was described as deeply intelligent, clinically depressed, a visionary, a person who would retreat for hours into privacy, a person who loved to read and did not enjoy physical labor, and someone who yearned to spend his time drawing, writing, and creating poetry. He spoke slowly and said, "I walk slowly but I never walk backward."

Lincoln's health issues are all typical vulnerabilities for Water types. He had hypotonia, or low muscle tone (also known as floppy baby syndrome), constipation, and probably Marfan syndrome, which affects the body's connective

42

tissue, which holds all the body's cells, organs, and other tissues together. He may have also had an extremely rare disease called multiple endocrine neoplasia, a genetic disorder that caused him to have long bones and excessive nerve-cell growth.

No one will ever know how much Lincoln suffered from some of his physical ailments. What we can be sure of is that never taking a vacation, being clinically depressed, and experiencing deep exhaustion doesn't help anyone, especially with an already taxed physical body, and particularly a Water. Loss of sleep, excess work, and lack of adequate water intake are major problems for Waters and can lead to emotional disturbances.

Lincoln's disturbances could have been helped by modern public utilities, such as clean drinking water. During the Civil War, the most popular drink was coffee, which was often made with dirty water. Caffeine and lack of water can both lead to dehydration, and dehydration leads to fatigue—which Lincoln suffered from. If you are a Water, take advantage of the easy-to-access clean drinking water that most of us have all around us, get plenty of rest, and stay balanced. We are lucky we live in an age when we can.

Waters Become One with Food

You may have heard the question "Do you eat to live or live to eat?" Waters live to eat. Comfort food doesn't even begin to describe their enthusiasm for food or capacity to indulge and enjoy. In fact, they can easily get hypnotized by food.

It was my last night at the beach. I had had a great weekend of writing, and to celebrate such productivity, I invited myself to dinner for crab legs and lob-

43

ster. Oh my! I'm so glad I said yes! I was the luckiest girl in the restaurant! I ordered the biggest plate on the menu and pigged out. I loved being alone and felt bad for all the people who were dining with friends and dates. I cracked open lobster and inhaled the tail whole. I pushed entire baby red potatoes into my mouth. I went through three ramekins of drawn butter. I managed to spray crab juice onto seats across from me. Butter was dripping off my chin and onto my chest. Pieces of ocean critters adorned my clothes (um, wasn't someone supposed to bring me a lobster bib?). I was in food bliss.

I sang along to a song from the band Heart that was blaring through the dining room speakers: "He's a magic ma-an, whoa, oh, oh, oh!" I didn't have to apologize for any of it, and I certainly didn't feel I was missing out. I got to observe the people, listen to conversations, enjoy the food, and be one with my thoughts, feelings—and crustaceans. I sat in an oversized, dimly lit booth and eavesdropped on private tales from other diners. I took time ordering and had whatever I wanted, including the biggest, most chocolaty dessert on the menu. I didn't have to clean my plate or take a doggie bag home. I didn't have to do anything out of obligation. For Waters, eating is less a social event than it is a chance to be comforted by food and to be alone with their thoughts.

Finding Balance as a Water

Most Waters love heavy sauces, rich creams, and large portions. But because their organs have to work overtime to process these dense meals, it's especially important to support the organs with regular physical movement and hydration.

The key with Water types is to not let themselves go through life feeling depleted energetically. When that happens, they tend to isolate themselves and become sedentary.

Waters also tend to get a little too comfortable at home. They can easily become one with the couch, even sitting in the same position for hours. It's important not to let this happen.

EXERCISE TO BALANCE WATERS
- Qigong
- Tai Chi
- Walking (even for ten minutes)
- Swimming

ENERGIZE YOUR WATER
- Stand up and stretch
- Have a good laugh
- Invite a Fire to dinner

BALANCE YOUR KIDNEYS AND BLADDER
- Acupuncture
- Acupressure
- Eden Energy Medicine

45

Eden Energy Medicine Exercise for Waters: Cross-Crawl Repatterning

This repatterning exercise resets the nervous system and supports crossover patterns in your body's energies, which are necessary for more energy and vitality. This exercise can also lift you out of depression or fuzzy thinking. As a Water you may need to do this twice a day for several days to feel a difference in your moods and energy level.

1. **HOMOLATERAL MARCH:** While standing, lift your left arm and left leg simultaneously. As you let them down, raise your right arm and right leg. Repeat several times.

2. **CROSS-CRAWL:** Lift your left arm and right leg simultaneously. As you let them down, raise your right arm and left leg. Repeat several times.

The Homolateral March and Cross-Crawl are essentially exaggerated walks. You can go back and forth several times, but always end the sequence with the Cross-Crawl.

Waters in Relationship

Noah and Hazel seemed to have a good relationship. Noah was kind and generous and a wonderful father to the children. He often bought Hazel flowers and offered to do the dishes or fold clothes. He never took Hazel for granted.

Everything seemed harmonious until Hazel wanted to talk about something deeper than the news of the day or what was happening at work. When she broached a subject that he considered at all difficult, Noah would clam up. He would say that there was nothing to talk about, even though there were a thousand words behind his eyes. If Hazel persisted, Noah would seem to get lost in his own head. His sentences would become short and vague. He seemed to be just waiting for the conversation to end so he could escape.

And yet Noah depended heavily on Hazel. He was even a little obsessive about how much he loved her. Without her, he would withdraw from society, stop taking care of himself, and lose confidence. He would become engulfed in fear.

If Waters have the freedom and time to talk about things that intrigue them, they will go on forever. However, if the conversation is something difficult and personal, or if things don't seem to be going smoothly, they tend to retreat deep inside themselves and become fearful. Waters can quickly personalize difficult issues and feel blamed and defensive, even when they aren't being blamed and have no reason to defend themselves.

If you're in relationship with a Water who retreats this way, you can gently give a timeline for when you need to talk. Let the Water know that you have something you would like to discuss and approximately how long you think it will take. For example, "Jim, I have something important that I would like to talk about. I think it will take about an hour of your time and I would like to know when, in the next couple of days, you have some time to talk with me." In this way, the Water will not feel ambushed and will be less likely to personalize the problem and more ready to listen.

If, on the other hand, the Water pressures you to talk immediately—already scared about the subject but eager to end the suspense—then you can talk immediately. However, the talk should be done in a private space that feels comfortable to both of you, and you should have enough time that you don't feel rushed. If the Water just wants to know what it's about, say what it is and ask for a time that works to talk in depth.

If your partner is a Water, she wants a deep relationship with enlightening communication. Small talk is boring, and if you aren't sharing more than light details about the weather or the particulars of your day, your Water isn't going to trust you or the relationship. At the same time, Waters need to feel safe enough to go deep.

Do You Know a Water?

The flowing, soothing, and gentle qualities of oceans, lakes, and rivers resemble the qualities of a Water person. But Water is also extremely strong. The Colorado River forged the Grand Canyon, one of the natural wonders of Earth, and the 2004 tsunami in the Indian Ocean was one of the most powerful natural disasters in history. As in nature, so it is with people.

You can recognize Waters in two ways: They will be either the most intriguing conversationalists you have encountered, or they will be sweet, curious, and playful like a little baby. Some Waters are both.

If you know someone who operates on her own time schedule, she is probably a Water or has strong Water tendencies. You may have tried different techniques to motivate her to join the world, but Waters join it randomly, without rhyme or reason. Sometimes it's like trying to tap a maple tree for the sap. When the sap finally flows, you might get small drops or an entire bucket. Like the sap, no amount of wishing Waters into action will make them do what you want them to do. Their willingness to participate in life comes from a mysterious place. Like mermaids who swirl in the world of magic and imagination, as long as they are allowed to stay in the flow of the Water, they are alluring, mesmerizing, and captivating. But if you remove them from their flow and force them to grow legs, they lose their creative powers.

Supporting and nurturing a Water is a tricky dance at times. They often grapple with shame and fear of exposure, and they often feel "unseen," so you may have to give them extra attention. Waters cannot be rushed through their restorative phases, either. They must have downtime to gestate their next project, embrace their next surge of energy, and mine for their most creative possibilities. By now you get it—the rhythm of Waters is slower paced than others. They need the space and time to resonate with their own rhythm.

49

You May Be a Water If . . .

If you have to read this book in parts, think about the content, read those parts again, think some more, and then take a break for a nice meal, you probably have Water in your personality—especially if you're reading this book *while* you're eating that meal.

You may be a Water if you search for meaning and importance in everything you do. Do you look for signs to know if something is right for you? Do you feel insecure and scared about life and about being your brightest self? Do you get lost in your high intellect because you want to know why certain things happen, where they start and end, and why we even exist? Do you want to have close friends but feel you're better off on your own because you don't want to burden people with your woes? Do people often tell you that you have an amazing mind? Do you feel that you move at a slower pace than everyone else? Do you feel scared of not being successful? Do you feel scared of becoming very successful? Do you feel fearful of what tomorrow may bring and how to navigate to your place in the world? Likewise, do you like to be silly with a loved one? Do you enjoy the pleasures of a little kid—like cuddling and tickling, camping out and eating yummy snacks with your closest friend or your partner? Do you yearn for someone else to do the hard work for you so you don't have to? Are you uncomfortable rushing, preferring to take time to enjoy your meals and your company?

If you are slowly nodding your head as you read this, then you are most likely a Water.

IF YOU THINK YOU ARE A WATER . . .

- ❍ Remember that you need downtime. Don't feel guilty about it. It is restorative and will make you a better person.
- ❍ Remember that you need playtime. Don't pass this up because you don't have the energy. You will probably get more energy once you start playing, and the play will make you more open and less fearful in the long run.
- ❍ Your motor runs a bit more slowly than others. You are not the sports car; you are the VW bus with the surf rack (really cool, but you might not win the race).
- ❍ Give yourself plenty of time to complete projects and be honest with people about the amount of time you need (always more than you think).
- ❍ If you've been playing video games or watching TV for two days straight, it's probably time to take a shower and leave the house. Take a break.
- ❍ Don't be so private, so secretive, and so silent that you lose friends. It doesn't benefit them or you. You may think it's mysterious, but it's really just annoying.
- ❍ Don't ever believe that people should be smart enough to read your mind if they love you or know you well enough. Believing that people should be able to read your mind will prevent any growth from happening in your relationships, and it will tick people off.

51

- When your partner says, "We need to talk," make time to talk. It doesn't have to be at that very moment, but it does need to happen within a day or two.
- Remember that there is more than just a beginning. Have faith and move forward.
- Don't let your body take the shape of the couch! Pick a form of movement or exercise that you like and do it three times a week. Your body will thank you.
- Beware of getting lost in your own stories and believing only them. Listen to other people's points of view and keep your mind open.
- Stay connected to human beings or other animals. Don't let paranoia keep you in a primitive state.

Water Personality Assessment Quiz

Take the following quiz to find out how strong you are in the Water element. Chances are that you're a combination of elements. This means some of these answers will be true for you and some won't. Accepting, understanding, and working with the elements that compose your personality are crucial to understanding the actions and motivations of others and being at peace with yourself.

Rate the following statements according to your tendencies. On a scale of 1

52

to 5, 1 is never true and 5 is always true. When you are finished, add up your score and compare it with your scores for the other elements in this book. A high score may mean that you have found your primary element. You are led by your primary element (or shared primary elements), which will dominantly reveal those respective traits in your personality, but you will be very influenced by your secondary, and to a lesser degree, third, fourth, and fifth elements. In certain circumstances you may draw on elements as a coping mechanism or strategy, but they may not be heavily present in your day-to-day life like your primary element(s).

1	2	3	4	5
Never True	Almost Never True	Sometimes	Almost Always True	Always True

Are You a Water?

UNDER STRESS I EXPERIENCE THE FOLLOWING:

_____ Sadness

_____ Laziness

_____ Fatigue

_____ Depression

_____ Hopelessness

_____ Lack of energy

53

_____ Tendency to retreat within

_____ Indifference

_____ Insomnia

IN GENERAL:

_____ Fear is the emotion that disables me the most.

_____ I'd prefer to stay at home with a good movie than go out and be sociable.

_____ I am wary of people and their motives.

_____ I am very introspective.

_____ I often lack stamina.

_____ I love naps and give them to myself whenever I can.

_____ I have lots of curiosity, and I can have a childlike wonder.

_____ I am often running late, but I still don't rush.

_____ In groups of people, I often keep my feelings and thoughts to myself.

_____ I am OK being anonymous.

_____ In class or in a group, I try to hide in the back.

_____ I love reading books, newspapers, and great articles in magazines.

_____ I am eager or feel driven to read or write daily.

_____ Ideas, more than people, stir my soul.

_____ I have brilliant ideas that stimulate others, and could change the world, but I need someone else to make them happen.

_____ I have a complex inner world that can be difficult for others to understand.

_____ I am fine with just a few good friends. I don't need a huge social life.

_____ I am slow to divulge my true feelings and careful of what I tell others about who I am.

_____ I want to uncover truths and mysteries.

_____ I yearn for meaning to this experience on Earth.

_____ I am very self-reflective.

_____ If I am disturbed while in a creative process, it is difficult for me to get back on track.

_____ I am comfortable being a follower and not a leader.

_____ When I feel "seen," I am more loving.

_____ I feel young and playful when I am loved.

_____ I am persistent.

_____ Above all else, I want to be loved by people.

_____ I go with the flow.

_____ I can get lost in the arts or creative processes.

_____ I am very private.

_____ Among friends, I can be very playful.

_____ I have been accused of being too secretive.

_____ I tend to believe that the world is a dangerous place and one needs to be careful.

_____ It takes me a while to really trust someone.

_____ Home is my safe haven, especially with my pajamas and popcorn.

_____ When I sit, I slouch and become one with the chair.

_____ When I walk, move, or dance, I flow like water.

_____ I don't love to exercise, but when I do, I prefer it to be something flowing and slow, like swimming or walking.

_____ Playing games like softball works well for me because the action isn't constant.

_____ When I speak, I often drone on for a long time.

TYPICAL PROBLEMS FOR WATERS:

_____ Sinking into isolation. It's common for people to have a hard time reaching me.

_____ I retreat deep into myself and feel resistant if people try to coax me out.

_____ I can become depressed and feel that I have no purpose.

_____ I lose energy easily and need to nap or sleep in order to restore it.

_____ I often feel suspicious of people, and I am aware of what they haven't done for me.

_____ When I am one-on-one, I can wax on eloquently for hours.

_____ I lose motivation easily.

_____ I shouldn't have to take care of me; I want someone else to do it.

_____ I feel paranoid at times.

_____ I suspect people and their secrets, yet I do not want my secrets exposed.

_____ I feel scared a lot.

_____ I feel paralyzed and frozen at times.

_____ Urgency is not in my nature, and I can lose track of time.

_____ I can get "icy" and be hard.

_____ I am more aware of how you're hurting me than of how I'm hurting you.

_____ I dwell on the past and its pain.

_____ **SCORE FOR WATER**

CHAPTER TWO

The Wood Personality
Getting Things Done

■

I never gave anybody hell. I just told the truth and they thought it was hell.
—HARRY S. TRUMAN, 33RD PRESIDENT OF THE UNITED STATES

WOOD ARCHETYPES:
   The Pioneer ▶ The Soldier ▶ The Visionary ▶ The Warrior

THE SEASON:
   Spring (bursting forth)

STRESS RESPONSE:
   Blame and accuse

FAMOUS PEOPLE WITH WOOD ELEMENT:
   Simon Cowell
   Bill Maher
   Rachel Maddow
   Pink

IF WOOD PEOPLE WERE ANIMALS:
   The Bulldog
   (strong and with a purpose)

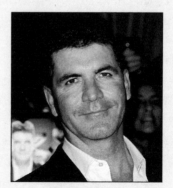

SIMON COWELL

Woods are fearless. They are like the sudden expansive growth of spring after a long, slow winter. They are like tree roots that push powerfully through solid concrete but are still rooted deep in the earth. Standing strong with a solid trunk, like an unbreakable oak tree growing toward the sky, Woods lead with a determination and will that surpasses all limits. Wood people see the bigger picture, find solutions, seek out the best in things, and make changes. They are strong, sturdy, stable, fearless, logical, reasonable, bold, independent, and unapologetic. They are also very fair-minded, and nothing upsets them more than injustices. This makes them powerful.

Woods live their lives with a singular focus on organizing the world. They are doers. They turn ideas into action, getting things done and then taking on the next project. Woods exude confidence and don't let much stand in their way. If they can imagine it, it will be done. They know what they want, are decisive, make things happen, and push themselves to the limit. They enjoy debates and arguments and are not easily swayed by the opinions of others. Once they make up their minds, there is little that can convince them that someone else's opinion is right. Woods know *they* are right, which acts as fuel for their strong drive but doesn't always bode well for their personal relationships.

Woods don't like to be fussy. They prefer low-maintenance haircuts that they don't have to spend time with every morning. Their clothing is simple and straightforward. Layers of clothing or flowing velvets, silks, and linens just seem to irritate a Wood. Woods prefer a simple top, jeans, and boots to a flowing shirt and silk parachute pants. "No-nonsense" is the fashion style for a Wood. Thinking about their clothing or hair products just distracts them from the work at hand.

60

Every element is led by a dominant emotion, and Woods are often led by anger. There is a subconscious simmering of anger that surges up fast for Woods, especially when they witness unfair situations or mistreatment of people.

Woods need to find a way to sway and bend like a willow tree, rather than stand rigid but then break. When Woods can find a way to combine their tenacity and strength with openness to their own vulnerability, the world will bow at their feet. Woods who stretch their minds, open their hearts, and evolve their spirits improve their already high-powered existence dramatically. And a few more simple steps will help them stay in balance once they've found it: Woods need to get plenty of sleep and rest, make sure they move their bodies every day, and rejoice in the company of friends and acquaintances instead of spending too much time alone with work.

When Woods are in balance, they are, of all the elements, the best coaches, the most resourceful implementers, the most decisive and clearest communicators, and the best at seeing the big picture. They do well under pressure, and if something goes wrong, they dig deeper and keep going. Pressure is a source of their drive, and they will also assist friends, family, and colleagues who are under pressure. They will be solid advocates and supportive cheerleaders. In other words, they'll have your back.

If Woods can learn how to slow down, mellow out, and gain compassion for others, they can experience resilient health and well-being, as well as enjoy productive careers and satisfying relationships. It helps Woods to have an upbeat partner to frequently give them a pat on the back or a high five. A quick acknowledgement lets Woods know that their hard work is noticed by the people they want to please the most.

Woods Grow Stronger Under Pressure

In 2008, I was happily pregnant, and I didn't want to give birth in a hospital. After years of being an advocate for friends and family who spent time in hospitals, I believed delivering at home with a midwife was just as safe, if not safer, than delivering in a hospital with a doctor and whole entourage of labor and delivery nurses. I also knew that I would need every ounce of evidence I could find to support a home birth. I had already heard people commenting that home births were not only dangerous, but selfish—putting the baby's health in danger—and hospitals were the only responsible place to give birth to a baby. I knew these were myths; nonetheless, I had to prepare myself for the onslaught of opposition. One doctor told me that if my home-birthed baby died, I would have only myself to blame. This type of pompous attitude is perfect fuel for a Wood to become even more grounded in her opinions.

As a Wood, it was natural for me to research my options thoroughly. Not only did I confirm that hospital births are not as safe as they are purported to be, but I found out that, as I suspected, home births might even be safer. A 2014 study in the peer-reviewed *Journal of Midwifery & Women's Health* confirmed that among low-risk women, planned home births had low rates of intervention and no more adverse outcomes for mothers and babies than institutional births. There might even be health benefits—not to mention cost savings—in having a home birth that reach far beyond those of the normal hospital delivery.

All my research was in service to my ideas: I believed that birth should be treated as a natural occurrence rather than a medical emergency. Along the way, I also learned that many aspects of pregnancy checkups are unnecessary. For example, routine prenatal vaginal exams are inappropriate because of the risk of infection and rupturing membranes. Obstetricians admit that they can find out anything they need to know in other ways (manual palpitation of the stomach, a woman's menstrual history, etc.). So while most women, not knowing any differently, accept these invasive checkups as a part of prenatal care, I managed my entire pregnancy without even a single one, as fit my ideals.

Doing research on the big business of natural and cesarean births in American hospitals, reading every peer-reviewed study I could get my hands on, and backing up my opinion with facts and statistics was a very Wood approach to my situation. I wanted to do things my way, make clear, rational choices, and stand firm in my convictions, even if this was not the easy route to take. I could not allow a hospital to hijack one of the most beautiful experiences I knew I'd ever have. And because of my research and insistence, I had the birth I wanted. I stuck to my choice of birthing at home, and I said no to all drugs and invasive procedures I was offered: no epidural, no labor augmentation, and no episiotomy. In the midst of intense pressure from friends, family, and the modern obstetrics system, most women do give up their freedom of choosing how they want to give birth, and sadly, many societies do not value a strong Wood woman. But I didn't give up. Not me. Not a Wood type.

Woods seem to be successful in whatever they attempt. The need to do more and do it *now*—it's in their DNA. Part of that success comes from their diligence. Woods know that personal responsibility and hard work are what it takes to get ahead. Is there a competition to enter? The Wood will take first place. This can look like good luck to the rest of the world, but Woods know that they've put in the time and the effort to produce excellence.

However, patience is not their strong suit. Ask a Wood to help with some-

63

thing that may take time, something that involves a lot of red tape, and their heads might just explode. Wasting time is almost unbearable and can feel like being thrown into a pressure cooker to them. Projects need to be done yesterday. Then again, if Woods have started a project with you, they will not leave you high and dry. Unfinished business can leave Woods restless and distracted, and they are repelled by the thought of personal failure and disloyalty.

Wood people are not interested in tasks at which they cannot excel. Woods want to be the best, and they want to get credit for doing a job well. The United States is a Wood country—it prides itself on being number one in the world with the biggest and best of everything. The United States has the most Olympic gold medals of any country, the largest consumer market on the planet, All-U-Can-Eat buffets that stay open twenty-four hours, four national sports whose winners are declared "World Champions" (most countries have one), and the largest, strongest military in the world. Many Woods volunteer to go to war.

It's all about control for a Wood type. If they don't feel in control of their daily life and focused on their short- and long-term goals, Woods will not be in the mood to interact. People might distract them from their goals. Woods who feel trapped or confined by a situation will move quickly to have the rules changed so that they can reinstate control and uphold their independence. Nina, a Wood friend of mine, says her worst nightmare is being out of control. She knows the result would be her entire world falling apart.

The Italian Mafia is a Wood organization. It isn't what we would call a healthy Wood organization, but it does incorporate many of the qualities that make up the Wood element: fierce loyalty, powerful leadership, unrelenting commitment to a cause, and an underlying river of anger. Mafiosi don't see themselves as murderers; they simply see themselves as close-knit networks of families who seek justice.

The Mafia family portrayed in the movie *The Godfather* contains a perfect example of dominant Wood (with secondary or tertiary Earth and Water elements). The godfather character, Vito Corleone, played by Marlon Brando, is the head of the Corleone family. He lives by the strict moral code of any macho gangster—reward loyalty and destroy anyone who gets in your way. He's ambitious and demands "respect" (fear). He prefers intimidation to murder as a first resort but uses his fearlessness and his reputation as a killer among killers to maintain control when necessary.

In the opening scene, a man comes to Corleone asking for protection. The man offers Corleone money. He begs. But Corleone feels that the man doesn't show enough respect, and so the scene intensifies. Not until the man kneels down, kisses Corleone's ring, and calls him godfather does Corleone agree to give protection. Respect and loyalty mean everything to a Wood.

Each element has complexities, and *The Godfather* offers a look at the darker side of Wood. On the positive side, balanced Woods are emotionally healthy, authentic, genuine, down-to-earth, generous, honest, ethical, and kind. Woods observe life in terms of what is fair, what is right, and what is wrong with the world. They can quickly draw up a strategic plan to fix whatever is broken. Seeing injustices and taking action to remedy them is one of their most honorable qualities. It distresses them when people don't get a fair shake. They believe that everyone should have equal opportunities. Typically, Woods help the underdog and will often go above and beyond for what they feel is an important cause or a person in need.

65

Woods Don't Give Up

In April 2016, the Treasury Department announced that by 2020 Harriett Tubman would grace the $20 bill. One of the most powerful abolitionists who didn't let beatings, whippings, and epileptic seizures deter her from her mission of helping slaves to freedom; she is finally getting long overdue recognition on a grand scale. In the 1800s, decades before the Civil War, runaway slaves would travel on foot at night, navigating by the North Star, to find new lives and safety in the North and in Canada. Leading the way was Harriet Tubman, who was a conductor on the Underground Railroad, a secret network of safe houses where runaway slaves could stay on their journeys to freedom. Harriet Tubman made thirteen trips from the South to the North, freeing between three hundred and one thousand slaves in ten years. She risked her life every day. And when a bounty of forty thousand dollars was put on her head for being a so-called slave stealer, she had to become even smarter and more focused.

On one of Tubman's trips, she went to rescue her husband, only to find that he had taken another wife while she had been away transporting injured, sick, and scared slaves through perilous nights. Other women may have allowed this unexpected curveball to devastate them and divert them from their plans. But Harriet was undeterred. She left her husband and his new wife and continued her work of finding slaves seeking freedom and escorting them to the North. One of the bravest people on the continent, she was called Moses by African Americans. Harriet Tubman was a Wood.

With a Wood, there are no head games: What you see is what you get. What a Wood is thinking is what will come out of his or her mouth. They speak the truth and don't mince words. On the downside, because Woods have very few filters, relationships can be tough. So are situations where they are expected to make small talk or be politically correct. It isn't against their nature to cross-examine people and see how far they can push them, with the motive of figuring out what makes people tick.

For a Wood, love doesn't make the world go around; honesty does. Speaking the truth is not a choice; it is part of their makeup. They see something and say exactly what it is, out loud for all to hear. They aren't concerned about hurting people's feelings or softening a blow. Thinking along those lines feels like a form of censorship to a Wood. You can imagine that when finesse or subtlety is necessary in business or love, Woods don't always know how to play that game, or they know exactly how to play that game, but they feel that playing games is just another form of dishonesty.

Woods Have a Point of No Return

In 1996, I was performing in the Polanco district of Mexico City. I was the exclusive belly dancer at a beautiful, upscale Lebanese dinner house with an eight-piece band and my own apartment, which connected to the dinner house through a maze of tunnels. The club catered to wealthy and well-known men and women of Mexico City. I even danced for a one-year-old baby millionaire on her first birthday. She sat high, cradled on a pedestal in a cream-colored bridelike dress with diamonds draping her body (and she cried the entire time I performed). There was also a famous international star who sat in a dark booth in the club to see my show multiple times and rumors swirled

67

about our affair. It was all very exciting and fun. On my days off, I would hop over to Acapulco to soak up the sun on the legendary beaches.

When my two-month contract was over, my boss sat me down in a small corner of the restaurant that was draped in lush vines and flanked by statues of Greek goddesses. He asked me to stay on for several more months and offered to increase my salary from $100 to $150 a night for my one-hour show. I told him thank you, but no. I was done.

We joked and laughed and told stories of my time in Mexico, like when a young man and his six-horn Mariachi band had serenaded me from the street below and woken up the entire neighborhood. My boss offered to double my pay to $200 per show. I told him again that I was done. We drank coffee, ate hummus, and regaled each other with descriptions of what makes a good performer. He offered to triple my pay to $300 per show. He said I was one of the best Middle Eastern dancers and he asked me what he could do to keep me in Mexico City.

My pay to perform at a restaurant in California was $35, with tips, so this was very good money he was offering. For a moment I imagined what I could do with $300 a night, per show (plus $100 to $300 in tips for each show) and how I would continue to be loved and admired by the community. It was very tempting.

And it was true that I loved Mexico City. It had been an adventure. I performed four nights a week, and on my days off I would travel to Guadalajara, Chiapas, and even Guatemala to see the sights. I roamed freely. A Wood person loves seeing and experiencing new things.

But as a strong Wood with a typically insatiable appetite for change and new adventure, my next goal was to perform in the Middle East. Nothing would stop me from pursuing that goal, not even $300 an hour plus tips for doing what I loved. I told my boss that really, truly, I was done.

Irritated, my Lebanese boss lectured me about certain rules in Mexico, like women being expected to be submissive and dependent. He warned me about the consequences of breaking social convention. A woman was expected to talk and respond in a congenial way with the authoritarian man, not stand firm in her convictions. As a Wood I have strong opinions that I have no problem voicing and turning into action. What I wasn't aware of—in the typical Wood way—was that I was about to offend his family, socially and culturally, by saying no to their patriarch. I don't always realize the ramifications of being forthright and honest with no filters, especially in social situations.

My boss was more than disappointed (and yet I felt an underlying respect and kindness from him too). Over the final days of my contract, I also felt slightly shunned by the family that had previously been so gracious to me. But as a Wood, I had made up my mind. That was that. I was done.

Wood Women: Powerful Rebels, Often Misunderstood

Woods, with their individuality, honesty, steadfastness, and unwavering confidence, wield great influence with defiant force. A Wood can be like a severe weather system barreling down on you, one that doesn't pause for you to find an umbrella. A pioneering Wood is an awesome power with which to contend.

However, a powerful Wood woman is perceived very differently from a powerful Wood man. Wood women have historically been viewed as rebels

69

and troublemakers, whereas Wood men have been seen as simply powerful, a quality that the most impressive men are expected to embody.

Wood women have a more difficult time than women of other elements. Their power can be intimidating to the societies they inhabit. Numerous Wood women leaders have been shunned because they spoke their minds and would not back down. Here are a few examples: Mary Wollstonecraft, who in the 1700s publicly proclaimed that women were more than possessions, had her reputation tarnished for nearly a century. Susan B. Anthony was thrown in jail for trying to vote. That didn't stop her from campaigning for equal pay for female teachers in 1846, and arguing for women's suffrage and the end of slavery. Emmeline Pankhurst was thrown in jail more than fifteen times in the late 1800s for working toward enfranchisement of British women. Rosa Parks was thrown in jail for resisting bus segregation and refusing to give up her seat to a white person in 1955. Janet Jagan became the president of Guyana in 1997 despite various attempts to remove her from leadership posts.

Strong Wood women have historically been misunderstood. People are not always comfortable with a woman being outspoken, blunt, assertive, or powerful, even today. These are traits we more comfortably associate—and respect—in strong men. But like it or not, Wood women are leaders for the world. They blaze new trails and they courageously get the work done.

While Water women are deeply entrenched in the latest novels and foreign films, Fire women are enjoying life and admiring each other's shoes, Earth women are cooking and baking for the local potluck, and Metal women are meditating and doing yoga, it is the Wood women who are busy creating policy and rewriting rules, laws, and regulations to help move the world forward.

Angie Dickinson—America's Sexiest Wood

When I was little, some of our closest family friends were the Bacharachs—as in the composer Burt Bacharach. Angie Dickinson—Burt's wife, who was voted one of the sexiest women in the world—is a Wood (with Metal and also Fire). Angie possesses all of the powerful qualities of a Wood—she is forthright, clear with her communication, clear with her boundaries, and blunt, with a wicked sense of humor. She is also generous and full of charity.

In 1974 Angie was cast in the first successful television show in American prime time to feature a woman in the title role—*Police Woman*. Not only that, but Angie was over forty, which was literally unheard of in Hollywood; there had never been a woman over forty to carry the lead in a successful dramatic series. Angie became one of the most famous female celebrities in the world—a household name—and was admired by women everywhere. She was one of the few women allowed into the famous group headed by Frank Sinatra known as the Rat Pack, and she often said that she was born "just one of the guys." Female Woods often say that they get along better with men than they do with women. As Angie so succinctly puts it, "I think like a man and I don't gossip like a woman."

Police Woman inspired a surge of applications from women to police departments throughout America. *Police Woman* is still referenced today when women apply to police academies. Angie was a role model for women on television that translated into the real world, and she has remained a role model to all who know her.

Angie has appeared in more than fifty films, won multiple acting awards, and received a star on the Hollywood Walk of Fame for her contribution to television. She has been a wife, mother, daughter, sister, and aunt—a prime example of a strong and devoted female Wood. After all of this success, she humorously quips, "I love that I was named one of the fifty sexiest women of the century. I would be content with that on my tombstone."

Woods and Emotion: Anger

In Chinese medicine, the organs governing the Wood personality are the liver and gallbladder, and the emotion is anger. The expression "That galls me!" describes a bitter or infuriating experience. The liver is the harmonizing organ in the body, and when liver chi (energy) is constricted—which is common with Woods—it is like a bottleneck inside the body. Whereas the Water, Fire, Earth, and Metal personality types all have real or imagined fears, Woods seem to bypass fear altogether and go straight to irritation and exasperation.

Anger can be a scary or negative concept for people in the West, where it seems to be taboo. Even admitting that you are angry can feel risky and unsafe, especially if you were taught that anger is an emotion that you should suppress. However, in traditional Chinese medicine, anger is seen as a friend who needs assistance. Anger out of balance can damage the liver, and liver problems can make us irritable (whether we are aware of them or not). Out of balance, Woods' anger will poison their relationships. In balance, it will fuel their determination. The goal is to foster healthy anger that isn't suppressed, a healthy liver and gallbladder, and healthy relationships.

You can help a frustrated Wood in your life to shift gears. Drop everything and take that person to a movie or play a game that distracts his or her intellect from thinking about how to fix the problems that are infuriating them.

72

Everyday fun as well as silly distractions will help to temper a Wood's frustration and irritation. Fires are good at this. They can help spark new, positive emotions in Woods and inspire them to leave their anger behind. The sooner Woods can accept that there is little in life that they can control, the healthier they will be emotionally and mentally.

If You Are Stuck in Anger

If you are a Wood stuck in an anger loop, get up from your desk, take a walk around the block, get off the phone, or walk away from the situation that is aggravating you. Get out of your space! More than any other element, Woods need to move. If they don't move, they tend to get stiff in their joints, bones, and emotions.

To be good partners and effective leaders, Woods need to find ways to soothe their irritation, speak mindfully, and practice kindness in expressing their frustrations. The path of growth for a Wood is to learn to show leadership without being authoritarian and to be competent without being arrogant.

Woods Don't Need to Shout to Make a Point

In church one day, my mom found herself sitting in a pew next to a father and his son. The son was a happy, restless boy about the age of six or seven, who was swinging his legs. The father was quiet and stern. He was trying hard to hear the sermon and control his son. It was obvious that the son's exuberance was making the father uncomfortable. He showed very little emotion as he sat, stiff and focused, with his eyes on the pulpit. But his growing tension was palpable. As the offering dish came through the pews, the father added some money and passed it to his son. The son excitedly shoved his hand into the dish and grabbed as much money as he could. In a severe tone, through gritted teeth and tight lips, the father said in a low, slow growl, *"Put the money back."* The father didn't even look at the boy. The son slowly but surely put the money back. Nothing else needed to be said.

Woods don't have to yell or shout to show their primary emotion. They simply remain calm, use words strategically, project their voice, pronounce their words crisply, and puff up their posture. For the most part, their anger isn't petty. They won't go ballistic just because they can't find their favorite shampoo on the shelves of their grocery store; they don't have time for that. Rather, Woods get angry when they feel out of control or when they observe injustices and disparity in life. Bullying in schools, lying in relationships, and laziness in the workplace are all intolerable to a Wood. They do not understand people who don't work hard, don't take personal responsibility, and treat others poorly. Woods will be direct and honest about these things. They feel honesty is the highest form of kindness.

DO!

- Do take time out every day to move and stretch.
- Woods can become very stiff, not only in their joints, but in their ways of reacting to the world.
- Moving and stretching will help keep your mind flexible.

Irritating a Wood is fairly easy if you are a person who is not accountable, who acts entitled, or who is ungracious. Anger can bubble up and boil over quickly for Woods, who will then question why more people aren't as ticked off as they feel. Doesn't everyone see what they see? As singer-songwriter Kasey Chambers says, "If you're not pissed off with the world, you're just not paying attention."

Balanced Woods have learned how to heal chronic anger and not let it dominate their lives. Many balanced Woods notice early on that anger can be fuel for them to get ahead and then they can release it. The anger actually feeds them and can help them achieve success, so they can then let the anger go.

Anger Can Fuel a Wood's Creativity

In the summer of 2003, I was participating in a gala show of Middle Eastern dance in Cairo, Egypt. Dancers from all over the world were performing, and they also sat in the audience watching the show. I had crossed paths with Safiya many times in different parts of the world. She was a Metal/Fire. Just as I was headed backstage to warm up, she lectured me about how I should approach her, and claimed that I needed to show more reverence to her in public. I was trying to get into the zone for my show, and as a performer she should have respected that. But even more galling was that she was telling me that I needed to bow down to her. Her Metal wanted to be treated like a queen, and her Fire made her almost hyper about it.

As the band started playing and an excited audience of more than three hundred people filled the ballroom, I became furious. In a matter of moments, the anger moved from my chest down to my feet and back up again all the way to my head. But rather than destabilizing me, it made me incredibly strong, confidant, and fearless. If I was nervous about performing before Safiya found me, I was not nervous now; rather, I was high on the intensity of being enraged. I was going to show the world that I was the best dancer in Cairo that night.

As the band played my entrance song, I pranced out onto the stage and danced as I had never danced before. My feet and hips were doing moves that they had never executed. It was as if someone else was dancing inside of me, and yet I was more in control than I had ever been onstage. I felt happy, self-righteous, superior, gorgeous, irresistible, and nine feet tall. The crowd went crazy! The band asked me to stay in Cairo and perform with them on a regular basis. A dance ethnologist in the audience gave me one of the best reviews she had ever written, saying that she had never seen moves like mine in her thirty years in the dance. And it was all because I was angry.

Healthy Woods know how to move anger through their bodies and use it to their advantage. The singer Pink says that anger and frustration are a motivator for her music. She has learned to use her anger in a healthy way and bring incredible singing and lyrics to people all over the world.

Healthy Woods learn how to let the anger flow when they get triggered. They learn to breathe into it and let it move through them productively, using it to fuel creative expression and clear communication. If they are out of balance or unable to take a break from their anger to cool down, their speaking style will be accusatory, and their driving energy can hurt, offend, or even intimidate people. They will be tempted to order, demand, berate, or snap at people. Instead, if they can take several deep breaths or step away from the situation that is upsetting them, the result will be better for both parties. With a softer tone and a calmer demeanor, Woods will be able to listen instead of exploding in frustration.

When Woods learn how to balance their anger, they can achieve mastery over their lives. When they're less exasperated because of limitations, restrictions, and delays, they won't feel the need to act like tyrants. They will be able to overcome obstacles with gentle determination, and their achievements will be grand.

The Strength of an Oak, the Flexibility of a Willow

Robin loved being a mom. It gave her a sense of purpose to know that she was responsible for raising a tiny person into an autonomous, self-reliant human being who just might change the world.

Her four-year-old son, Ronan, was very intelligent, and Robin often had to remind herself that he was only four. There were days, though, when Robin's frustration overpowered her reason. "Ronan, please listen to me." "Ronan, please work with me." "Ronan, we're late, so please help me put on your shoes!" If she had to repeat herself one more time, she thought her blood might boil over.

As a Wood, Robin had always felt she knew how to control everything, from the way the house looked to how to get people to listen to her when she spoke. Now there was a little boy who tested every bit of control, grace, and patience she had. Ronan was a power child who wanted to be the boss and get whatever he desired in the moment. From the day Ronan took his first steps, Robin seemed to have little control over this little man, who wanted to be king of the household.

In the past, logic had helped Robin stay centered, as it does with most Woods, but logic can do little with a child who doesn't understand why he can't eat ice cream all day and have all the toys in the store when they're right there for the taking. Robin often felt like screaming at the top of her lungs and throwing things. Luckily, she was familiar with her Wood tendencies, especially under stress. She knew she had options.

One day, when Ronan was standing defiantly with his fists clenched, screaming because he wanted to play ball in the house, Robin took a time-out. It wasn't her first instinct. Her first instinct was to give him an ultimatum, take his ball away, and sit him in a chair where she could keep an eye on him. But on this day she excused herself from the room and took a break. She told Ronan she was feeling very upset and needed a few moments alone. She went into the next room, keeping the door open so Ronan wouldn't feel shut out. During her break, Robin shut her eyes (Woods are governed by their eyes, so shutting them and resting them has a very positive impact), and she did some deep breathing. Within minutes she thought of kind ways to speak to Ronan. Shouting never reached him anyway.

78

Robin returned to the room where Ronan was still fuming. She got down to his level and told him she understood his anger. Ronan shouted, "Yeah, I'm *really* mad, Mommy! I want to play ball in the house!" Robin used reflective listening, a technique to foster understanding: She told Ronan she understood that he wanted to play ball in the house and that she imagined it was fun for him to bounce the ball around. She also told him softly about how the ball could break things, especially the things he loved.

After some silence, the tension began to subside and Robin talked to Ronan about his options. Ronan could roll the ball on the floor slowly instead of throwing it overhand; he could play ball in the front yard or the backyard; or he could find another game that they could play together. Ronan's anger began to subside because his mother was no longer being dictatorial or unyielding.

Robin noticed that every time she was inflexible and rigid, she and Ronan would have a power struggle. Practicing reflective listening, offering options, and taking breaks when her anger arose were ways she could manage her strong feelings. It worked not only with kids, but also adults. It was often the difference between becoming rigid like a rock or bending and swaying with the grace of a willow tree but the strength of an oak.

Helping a Wood Stay Flexible

Helping Woods to bend, sway, and stay flexible is as simple as reminding them of what they are doing well. They will not only do those things better, but other things will get better too. Praise—even a small amount—will create a positive ripple effect for a Wood. To quote a fortune cookie: "Correction does much, but en-

79

couragement everything." Similarly, suggestions for improvement need to be presented as *suggestions*, because Woods have usually worked very hard to get where they are, and they want people to notice. They set high standards for themselves and take responsibility seriously, so it's wise to not focus on what a Wood has done wrong but to present suggestions "for the good of the relationship." As soon as they feel blamed, Woods are likely to get triggered and feel defensive.

Woods and the Body

Most Wood-dominant types are stocky, solid, and strong in their physical body, with broad, square shoulders. They build muscle with less effort than others, and they look grand even if they are small in stature. Their walk is like a march, focused and determined in the direction of their destination. When out of balance physically, Woods may experience muscle spasms, side-of-the-head headaches, numbness, vision problems, stiff joints, arthritis, and autoimmune diseases.

Perhaps more than any other element, Woods need to eat whole, healthy foods and not indulge in alcohol and other drugs. The liver has more than five hundred functions, including cleaning the blood, metabolizing drugs, controlling the immune response, regulating fats and sugars, and absorbing what cannot be digested (including emotions). The gallbladder makes and stores bile but also rules decisions. Just as a Wood person is decisive and constantly seems to be discriminating between what is right and wrong, so too does the liver and gallbladder. Both the liver and gallbladder help determine how many nutrients will go to the rest of the body and how many will stay behind in storage.

80

In the spring of 2014, I had spontaneous bleeding from my hands, feet, and nose. My eyes were puffy and irritated. My back hurt so badly, I thought it might be broken. I am a very healthy person, so this health crisis didn't make sense to me. I started going through checklists of what might be going on. How often was I exercising? How much sleep was I getting? How many processed and preservative-laden foods was I eating? I went to visit an Ayurvedic doctor and filled out her checklist too.

Did I smoke? No.
Take drugs? No.
Drink alcohol? Rarely.
Take pharmaceutical medications? No.
Exercise? Yes.
Drink plenty of water? Yes.

The checklists confirmed that I had led a very healthy lifestyle for more than forty years. But there were a couple of things that tipped the scales in the direction of ill health. They had a much more significant impact on me than they might have had on others, simply because I am primarily a Wood type. Traveling around the world for a living made me rely heavily on fast food for my meals. Fast foods are filled with preservatives, additives, solvents, and other chemicals. The liver and gallbladder have a very difficult time processing these toxins. They should never be in our bodies in the first place. The combination of being addicted to Jack-in-the-Box tacos and working long hours all day, every day, was starting to take a toll.

Would this routine wipe out the other Five Element types if the rest of their

81

lives were relatively healthy? Maybe not, but Woods are ruled by the liver and gallbladder, meaning that they are more affected by the functions of these organs than other personality types. The liver is involved in all of the ailments I was experiencing, from the storage of blood, to pain and stiffness in my tendons, to eye puffiness (liver energy opens into the eyes through the liver meridian, an energy pathway in the body). I had to find a way to get myself well without the use of pharmaceutical medications, which would just wreak more havoc on my liver and gallbladder.

Over the next year, I followed an Ayurvedic diet of bone broth, room-temperature water, and swigging the occasional glass of castor oil. It helped immensely in getting me back on the road to health.

A Wood can help the liver by cleansing it. The liver can become toxic through poor dietary habits, because anything that you ingest has to be processed by the liver. That goes for aspirin, caffeine, pharmaceuticals, sugar, heavy meals—everything—even stress. The liver works very hard to detoxify and eliminate what it perceives as bad for your system. Therefore, cleansing your body—even very simply, by eating organic fruits and vegetables and eliminating heavy, dense foods for short periods of time—gives your liver a chance to rest.

Doing occasional juice fasts with high water content (preferably alkaline water) is very good for the liver. There are also many herbs to aid the liver, including Oregon grape root, which clears the liver of toxins, and milk thistle, which promotes bile flow. Both of these can be taken in tea or capsule form.

However, the real key is for Woods to practice healthy eating every day. Most important is to eat small meals of unprocessed foods and beverages. Woods need to remember that large meals (and a lack of exercise) force excessive bile production, which stresses the liver. In addition, a high-volume diet puts

82

unnecessary stress on all of the organs. Eating small amounts of organic, un-processed, and free-range foods, including plenty of fruits and vegetables, is a good way for most Woods to maintain a healthy liver. It's also good for the gallbladder.

Supporting the liver and gallbladder with acupuncture and acupressure will also help Woods live long and energetic lives.

YOUR LIVER AND GALLBLADDER LOVE THESE FOODS

- Lemons
- Dark leafy greens
- Salmon
- Almonds

YOUR LIVER AND GALLBLADDER LOVE THESE HERBS

- Dandelion root
- Milk thistle
- Peppermint
- Oregon grape root

Movement for Woods

Woods excel at martial arts, weight training, and rhythms of certain synco-pated, choppy dance styles, like break dancing and hip-hop. But they also need to limber up to move lymphatic fluid and lubricate muscles and bones, rather than building mass and bulk. Yoga, stretching, and walking will help a Wood stay flexible in body and mind. Breathing techniques will lower stress. If a Wood can breathe out her anger in mind-body practices like Qigong, Tai Chi, and so on, Woods can shift their interactions from confrontation to empowerment.

Unfortunately, slower exercises, like yoga—and even worse, stillness practices, like meditation—can feel like a joke to a Wood. Woods often don't feel that they need personal growth. As far as balance goes—well, that can just take too long. Because of their impatience with taking care of themselves, they are in danger of becoming hardened, bitter people. Slower mind-body practices are precisely what a Wood needs to return to balance.

EXERCISE TO BALANCE WOODS
- Martial arts
- Speed walking
- Stretching

CALM YOUR WOOD
- Stop and breathe
- Take four or five slow, deep breaths
- Shut your eyes
- Rest your vision

BALANCE YOUR LIVER AND GALLBLADDER

- Acupuncture
- Acupressure
- Eden Energy Medicine

Eden Energy Medicine Exercise for Woods: Blowing Out the Anger

Becoming more viscerally familiar with anger makes space for healthy assertiveness. The following exercise helps to move stuck Wood energy—including rage—out of the body and free congested energies. Plus, it feels great!

1. Stand up straight. Put your arms in front of you, bend your elbows slightly and make fists. Have the insides of your wrists facing up and take a very full breath.
2. Swing your arms up behind you and over your head. Reach way up.

85

3. Then rush your arms down the front of your body as you emphatically release your fists. Let out your breath and your emotions with a whoosh sound or any other powerful sounds that come naturally. (You can even say a name if you're mad at someone and you want to release your anger toward that person.)

4. Repeat these steps and movements several times. The last time, bring your arms down in a slow and controlled manner, blowing your breath out of your mouth as you go.

Finding Balance as a Wood

Sheryl loved working. She felt alive when she had projects to accomplish and companies to grow. She often joked that she could write a book called *The Joy of Stress*. Being under pressure was something she actually looked forward to, the way other people look forward to a good meal. It fed her. Sheryl wanted to do it all, and she wanted to do it yesterday. People were impressed by the speed at which she accomplished massive projects that seemed to bury others. The expression "consider it done" captured the essence of who Sheryl was.

Cunning and independent, Sheryl sensed opportunities when others saw nothing, and she was always right, leaving others scratching their heads and wondering how they'd overlooked what she had seen so clearly. She also knew how to fix problems. She was incredibly successful, looked great, was always on time, rose to the top of a high-powered financial institution in New York City, and had an immaculate penthouse.

86

Success was Sheryl's middle name, but she wanted more. She wanted a fabulous boyfriend (the concept of marriage and children was boring to her) and time to relax. She had all of the ingredients to get both. However, when she stopped pushing herself into the next project, she found herself scattered, disoriented, and lost. Constantly doing was addictive. In reality, the holidays and vacations that she longed for spun her into a place of pessimism, irritability, and agitation. Slowing down was like stopping a drug cold turkey.

To try to relax when she wasn't working, Sheryl would drink wine and eat sugary, fatty foods. Then she would often fast on water and fruit to make up for the overindulging. Sheryl wasn't overweight, and a few drinks once a week wasn't risky behavior for her, but the inconsistencies in her eating, her constant drive, and the burden of being incredibly ambitious took a toll on Sheryl.

Coming into balance was a chore. Finding ways to be engaged but not burned-out was one of the most difficult tasks Sheryl had ever faced. The obligation to rest, read, eat right, visit friends, take leisurely walks, and breathe was not fun for her. She would've rather spent a fourteen-hour day at the office than get a massage and meditate. Relaxing almost felt threatening. Over time, however, Sheryl stayed with it and became healthier in body and mind. She developed more empathy for others and learned to laugh at herself. She started to smile with joy from her heart instead of pasting on a smile that was supposed to tell people she was happy. She became well rested, looking ten years younger. Sheryl became physically, mentally, and emotionally flexible and thereby gained more peace. The change probably saved her life.

87

Woods in Relationship

Dennis loved Diane deeply. The sun rose and set on her. Diane loved the fact that Dennis gave her the freedom to be herself and voice all of her strong opinions. If she saw something on the news that bothered her, she could talk with Dennis about how mad it made her. If they were at a restaurant together and the meal wasn't to her liking, Diane would speak up and let the management know, and Dennis supported that type of honesty, which some partners might find embarrassing. If Dennis and Diane were arguing, Diane would express herself freely about how she disagreed with Dennis and why. Diane could be her authentic self around Dennis.

One day while Diane was talking about inequality between the sexes, Dennis looked at her with tears in his eyes and softly asked, "Why do you always have to be so angry?" Diane had no idea what Dennis was talking about. She didn't feel angry. She felt empowered and justified. She also felt a great responsibility to speak up and overcompensate for all the people who weren't saying anything about injustice. To Diane, people who didn't speak up were cowards, and the silence was a form of dishonesty. But Dennis needed a break from the constant rage that Diane seemed to have at the world. Dennis needed a rest from Diane's Wood.

Being in partnership with a Wood can feel like a lot of pressure. In fact, *being* a Wood can feel like a lot of pressure. Woods will want their partners to listen to their tales of annoyance and irritation regarding people and events from the day to help relieve their internal pressure. But their partners can get very tired of the venting.

It is important for Woods to find good friends (or siblings) to whom they can air their complaints. They need to remind themselves that most partners do not find anger attractive. Woods almost never realize how angry they sound, so they need to check themselves. If you are a Wood, ask yourself how much you've been airing your grievances and for how long.

To Woods, it's very simple: They announce who and what has angered them, they rectify it, and then they get back to work. Meanwhile, their partners are often still dealing with the impact of what can feel like a battering storm. Woods need to remember that most people need some transition time from the intensity of their emotion and some reassurance that things are actually OK. When Woods express anger it doesn't mean they aren't happy people or don't enjoy life and companionship, but this is not always clear to others.

In companionship, Woods expect a lot not only of themselves, but also of you. Prepare to have the bar raised! There will be no sleepwalking through a relationship with a Wood. They want sincere and direct communication; they will give honesty and they expect it. If you are a person who closes down easily or gets intimidated by others, a Wood may think you're being sneaky, weak, or dishonest.

In relationships with Woods, it's important to clearly convey that you have your own rhythm and that it may be slower than theirs. Let Woods know that just because you ponder and process doesn't mean you don't want to communicate and reach solutions. Giving them information can go far in helping them have patience with your way of being. Being honest with them, even if you stumble through your words, is the golden ticket to maintaining peace with a Wood.

Woods really can be fun, funny, and romantic *if* they can relax. A partner who has a sense of humor or who has a lot of Fire can usually lure a Wood away from his or her desk to unwind. Most Woods are very driven in their work, personal causes, and daily lives, so a good distraction works well. Share a joke with them or invite them to a happy hour (but watch the alcohol)! If you're wondering how to make Woods happy or really turn them on, just present a challenge or good debate. They need to be unhooked from whatever has hooked them. After acknowledging them and making sure they feel heard, use distraction to help them find their joy and laughter.

Miles Copeland—a Formidable Wood

Miles Copeland has been called a Svengali and a maverick. He is one of the most influential figures in the music industry and has had a career that has spanned forty years. Miles was raised in the Middle East by his father, who was one of the founders of the CIA (and an arranger and trumpet player for the Glenn Miller Orchestra), and his mother, who was in Special Ops during World War II. In London during the seventies, Miles worked with the Sex Pistols, the Clash, Blondie, the Bangles, Squeeze, and his brother Stewart's band, the Police. He managed Sting through seven blockbuster albums. He founded I.R.S. Records and had hits with REM, the Buzzcocks, the English Beat, the Cramps, Fine Young Cannibals, Wall of Voodoo, and the Go-Gos. In the late nineties, Miles started combining Arabic music with Western music and had huge success with the song "Desert Rose." In 2002 Miles formed the Bellydance Superstars, a dance troupe hailed as "The New Riverdance" by the London *Sunday Times Magazine.*

If you Google Miles Copeland, you will find an endless list of his accom-

90

plishments and amazements. After spending more than a year traveling with him and working for him, I know that a great deal of his success is due to his strong Wood element. He has all the bold qualities of a Wood—he is audacious, fearless, brassy, and bold—as well as discourteous, ill-mannered, brusque, and insensitive. He is also undaunted by anyone's reaction to him that is less than positive or kind.

In 2004 I had spent three months traveling around North America on a toiletless bus with twelve other women, all hired by Miles to change the image of belly dance in the West. We were the Bellydance Superstars. Miles told me he wanted me to continue the tour to Barcelona for a month and I jumped at the chance. However, I didn't want to perform the numbers I had been performing. I wanted to do a solo *zambra mora* (Moorish party) piece. This was called the "forbidden dance" of the Moors (who conquered Spain beginning in 711) because it was banned along with all other aspects of Moorish culture after the Christian Reconquest. Miles told me he wanted to see the dance and asked me to travel to his home in Hollywood and perform for him and his wife. Traveling to one of the most historic parts of Hollywood, near the famous Runyon Canyon, was my cup of tea (as someone with a lot of Water element, I love history). After passing through the giant gates, I found myself amid burgundy velvet antique furniture and stained glass in the historic home that formerly belonged to Raymond Burr. Miles's driver moved the antique furniture out of the way, and I danced my heart out, with splits, kicks, and Turkish drops and then waited with bated breath to hear what Miles thought. He loved it! I would be doing *zambra mora* in Spain! That was it. I drove home to San Diego and started packing for Barcelona.

Opening at the historic Teatre Victòria to more than eight hundred people was exciting! I leaped and twirled across the stage, nailing my layouts, back-bends, and drops. My piece ended to thunderous applause, but Miles stormed backstage to tell me my routine didn't work. He yelled into my dressing room that he was canceling it from the show! I would still perform all my other numbers and stay in Spain for the month, but my *zambra mora* would be nixed. I followed Miles through the wings of the stage, reminding him that he had loved my routine back in Hollywood, and so did his wife. He said that it was different in his living room in Hollywood, but this was a large stage in Spain. In Spain he decided the routine wasn't working and he didn't like it! Case closed.

Moments like this with Miles were common. He said how he felt with no filters and no time for reassurance. Around Miles you learned to take what he said and move on. It was cut and dried, with no extra padding. With Miles I often felt like a crawling baby in an un-baby-proofed home. A sharp table corner in the eye or sudden tumble down a staircase could come when I least expected it. I had to learn to flow with a person who was very unflowing.

I thanked the heavens for Miles's bits of Fire and Water elements, which often appeared as a fun-loving dad, a supportive uncle, and a fun, close friend. He got sweetly excited over coconut ice cream, champagne parties for the cast and crew, and new pillows for our tour bus. He was loveable and even playful at times. But his Wood was what ran the ship, wielded his power all over the world, and tended to dominate over any other elements that lived in his soul. His Wood taught me much about showbiz and is, after all, what helped Miles book contracts all over the world and what made him the mighty Miles Copeland.

Woods Need to *Do*

Woods are workaholics, and many of them are taskmasters. People very strong in Wood are opinionated and aggressive, rarely taking time to relax and have fun. They will probably order you around. However, there are ways to get a Wood away from work, rules, and rigidness. Woods need to *do things*, so if you're in a relationship with a Wood, offer something to plan. For example, let her organize the next vacation. That way, it will be sure to happen, and she'll feel productive, feeding her sense of value and importance. You can even negotiate a few hours of lying on the beach or being lazy by the pool if you tell her she can plan an entire city tour or a night out on the town. Give her a challenge and she'll meet it. She'll even get it done early.

Do You Know a Wood?

By now you probably know if you have a Wood in your life or if you're one yourself. When a person starts to outreason you on almost everything, you won't have a doubt. Woods don't have time for fluff. The words they choose have great impact, and they have an impressive knack for distilling issues down to a fine, sharp point (which can sometimes feel insensitive and intrusive).

On the other hand, as friends or lovers they are steadfast and reliable. Loyalty and honesty are extremely important to Woods. Though they may not want to sit around a campfire singing "Kumbaya" with you, they will take your call ten years after you thought your relationship was over (they will be candid at the time about why it ended, of course). They will be there for you when you're down-and-out.

If you want a straightforward, honest point of view, introduce yourself to a Wood. You may not convince her to go to a party or join your social circles, but she will have your back when you need an ardent supporter, be the first to stand up for you if you are ever wronged, and protect you if you are ever confronted with danger. (She will also let you know if your butt *does* look big in that dress or if your hair really *is* thinning on top.) Woods can become quite dynamic and ferocious when their loved ones are treated poorly by others. Being bullied? You need a Wood by your side.

Remember, Woods want you to see how great they are, and they want the acknowledgment and credit for being great. Don't ever tell your Wood partner, "It wasn't very good, but you'll do better next time." This will make a Wood feel humiliated and lost. Woods need to hear that they were good and that you know they'll do even better, because you know how hard they work.

You May Be a Wood If . . .

You may be a Wood if you yearn for truth, justice, honesty, and equality. Does anger propel you into action? Do you feel secure in who you are, confident in your choices, and unapologetic for decisions you have made? Do you work swiftly and efficiently for long hours until the job is done? Are you a loyal friend but don't have a lot of time for social niceties? If you are reading this and trying to high-five yourself shouting "Yes!" and standing tall, then you are most likely a Wood.

IF YOU THINK YOU ARE A WOOD . . .

○ Remember that most people are not like you. They are governed by different elements and follow their own inclinations to success and happiness. This doesn't mean that they're flaky, irresponsible, or stupid.

○ You probably have some of the quickest thinking processes and are one of the most efficient workers in your milieu. Most people process at a slower pace. Remind yourself that others may need to sit with their thoughts and decisions for longer than you do.

○ Give people the benefit of the doubt—and more time than feels comfortable.

○ Avoid being so convinced that you are right, so firm in what you believe, and so confident in your own abilities that you truly don't believe that you need people. Chopping people out of your life will eventually hurt you.

○ Don't be blinded by your efficiency and perfectionist nature. To the rest of the world, your efficiency is called *impatience*, and it can stress people out.

○ Discard the assumptions. For instance, when you see people playful, relaxed, or down-and-out, don't assume that they're lazy.

○ Remember that to others it looks as though you have it all together. When you don't have it all together, it's helpful for people in your life to hear about your challenges.

95

○ Vulnerability can be your greatest power, because it connects you back to people when you've become a bitter solo player, which can happen when there is a lot of anger.
○ Use "I" language instead of "you" language—"I'm feeling hurt," not "You've made me angry."
○ Listen to understand, not just to respond.
○ Do something fun or soothing at least once a week. Take a dance class, chill out with a good book, go to a movie. Do anything but go back to your computer.

Wood Personality Assessment Quiz

Take the following quiz to find out how strong you are in the Wood element. Chances are that you're a combination of elements. This means some of these answers will be true for you and some won't. The quiz results will tell you how dominant your Wood characteristics are within you. Accepting, understanding, and working with the elements that compose your personality are crucial to understanding the actions and motivations of others and being at peace with yourself.

Rate the following statements according to your tendencies. On a scale of 1 to 5, 1 is never true and 5 is always true. When you are finished, add up your scores and compare them with your scores for the other elements. A high score may mean that you have found your primary element. You are led by your primary element (or shared primary elements), which will dominantly reveal those respective traits in your personality, but you will be very influenced by your secondary, and to a lesser degree, the third, fourth, and fifth elements. In certain circumstances you may draw on elements as a coping mechanism or strategy, but they may not be heavily present in your day-to-day life like your primary element(s).

1	2	3	4	5
Never True	Almost Never True	Sometimes	Almost Always True	Always True

Are You a Wood?

UNDER STRESS I EXPERIENCE THE FOLLOWING:

_____ Exasperation

_____ Impatience

_____ Muscle tension and tightness

_____ Frustration and irritation

_____ Anger

_____ Inability to relax

_____ Eyestrain or puffy eyes

_____ Resentment

_____ Restlessness

97

IN GENERAL:

_____ I am assertive and clear about where I stand.

_____ When I have made a decision, it is very difficult to get me to change my stance.

_____ I want to have full control over every aspect of my life.

_____ I see goals, and I need to accomplish them.

_____ I see the future and what it takes to get there.

_____ I find it very difficult to not constantly focus on my vision until I succeed at it.

_____ I enjoy organizing my environment.

_____ I prefer structure and plans to happenstance.

_____ I am obsessed with completing items on my to-do list.

_____ I feel an undeniable need to stand up for people who are treated unfairly.

_____ I have a purpose when I work, and I always find ways to do more.

_____ I am good at setting priorities and getting them done.

_____ I find it hard to relate to people who don't tell the truth.

_____ I have a reputation for being solid and dependable.

_____ I like to compete, and I often feel competitive in noncompetitive situations.

_____ I care about people, but I don't overworry about hurting their feelings.

_____ I am grounded in reason and facts.

_____ I hate being late, and I hate when others are late. There is rarely an excuse for it.

_____ I cannot stand when people waste my time.

_____ I can be incredibly effective when I'm angry.

_____ I have a gift for seeing the big picture when others seem to be mired in the details.

_____ I need to do things my own way and always have an opinion about your way.

_____ I rarely turn down a good argument or debate. Conflict doesn't scare me.

_____ I work very hard, so you'd better have a very good reason for criticizing me.

_____ I am courageous and determined when I feel strongly about a cause.

_____ I am fiercely independent, and I will not be pushed around.

_____ I am confident in most anything I take on.

_____ I have no problem stating my personal boundaries.

_____ I have an indomitable will to succeed.

_____ I always find my inner strength when in difficult situations. I perform well under stress.

_____ I am comfortable in my skin, and I feel a great connection to self.

99

_____ I am compassionate and very generous if the need is genuine.

_____ I believe honesty is the ultimate kindness.

_____ I am good at seeing what needs to be done, and I want it done yesterday.

_____ I am an effective communicator.

_____ When I fail at something, I take responsibility and I do everything I can to fix it.

_____ When I commit to a project or person, I am very loyal.

_____ I am easily offended by people with inappropriate behavior and bad form.

_____ I have a dry and sometimes sarcastic sense of humor.

_____ I am a hard worker, and I expect others to work hard too.

_____ I enjoy doing powerful kickboxing and karate-like movements when exercising.

TYPICAL PROBLEMS FOR WOODS:

_____ I find it difficult to relax.

_____ I can easily lose my temper.

_____ I can be judgmental and critical of others.

_____ I can be very stubborn and stuck in my ways.

_____ I can be uncompromising.

_____ I tend to see what's wrong instead of what's right.

100

_____ I can be sharp-tongued.

_____ It is difficult for me to delegate.

_____ I can become addicted to my work.

_____ I can believe that I am better than everyone else.

_____ I hate to lose.

_____ I have a point of no return with people.

_____ I become very frustrated if I am limited from stating my opinion.

_____ If I am not allowed to express my anger, I can explode.

_____ I get irritated if someone tries to slow me down. I have things that need to get done.

_____ **SCORE FOR WOOD**

CHAPTER 3

The Fire Personality
Enjoying the Ride

*If you're going to be able to look back on something and laugh about it,
you might as well laugh about it now.*

—MARIE OSMOND, PERFORMER

FIRE ARCHETYPES:
The Wizard ▶ The Unconditional Lover ▶ The Comedian ▶ The Life of the Party

THE SEASON:
Summer (expansion)

STRESS RESPONSE:
Panic

FAMOUS PEOPLE WITH FIRE ELEMENT:
Ellen DeGeneres
Jim Carrey
Bette Midler
Robin Williams
Tom Cruise

IF FIRE PEOPLE WERE ANIMALS:
The Dolphin
(happy, social, and fun-loving)

ELLEN DeGENERES

103

Fires are the torches that transform dense custard into sugar-topped crème brûlée. They are the orange icing on the dry English biscuit that makes it the best darn cookie you've ever eaten. They shake their pepper on the mediocrity of life and every experience becomes a spicy celebration of colors, sounds, joy, and pleasure. They burn away the status quo.

Fires are carefree, but that doesn't mean they don't care. They are simply present in this moment. More than any other element, they are in the *now*. They are not tethered to what happened yesterday or what may happen tomorrow. They are all about the excitement of this moment. Whereas Waters tend to resonate with history, Woods clearly see tomorrow, Earths are comforted by nostalgia, and Metals try to embrace the present but drift toward the future, it is Fires who truly live for the moment, especially if there is pleasure and people are involved.

People are drawn to Fires because of their zest for life and contagious positive spirit. Fires are demonstrative and playful, not scared to hug, touch, and be in other people's personal spaces. However, Fires change frequently and are always finding new interests and desires. They truly love everybody and will quickly gravitate to where they feel the most pleasure and passion. This can be hard on others, especially when a relationship begins in an exciting way, and then—poof!—the Fire is gone, on to the next adventure.

Fires Are the Life of the Party

Maddie, living in London, invited us on a trip to Morocco. My mom and I accepted, planning to stay in Marrakech for one week before moving on to the coastal town of Essaouira. I had traveled in Arabic countries when I was performing on the belly dance circuit, but Morocco is different—a rich mix of Berber, Arabic, North African, and European influences—so my mom and I read all the travel guides to get familiar with the culture and learn how to respect the local customs before we arrived.

We followed the suggestions for dressing modestly while walking around and visiting mosques. It was easy enough to wear long sleeves, cover our cleavage, and don veils. But the Marrakech souks (marketplaces) made us nervous. We had read about vendors harassing, following, and intimidating tourists. Other Westerners told us to prepare to get totally lost and be on guard at all times. We were warned: "No eye contact, close your ears, and keep your sunglasses on. Hold each other's arms tightly, and don't let each other out of your sight. You are walking cash machines." Plus donkeys, mopeds, carts, and bikes would all squeeze into the tiny lanes together, causing confusion and making us easy targets.

I asked a friend who had traveled there before if we should avoid the souks altogether. "Only if you're timid or female," she said. Mom, Maddie, and I talked about it for many days and decided we would disregard her comment. *We had to go to the souks!* They *are* Marrakech! With snake charmers, Gypsies, tanneries, and just about everything you ever wanted to buy, from exotic perfumes and spices to Berber jewelry and dolls, we knew that visiting the markets would be one of the most amazing experiences we would ever have. There was no way around it.

So we prepared to be lost and bombarded. We practiced role-playing and saying *no* in low, deep voices while marching forward. In the moments before we entered the largest traditional Berber souk in Morocco, we entwined our arms and stood tall.

But before we could enter the dark, crooked pathways, Maddie broke ranks and strolled happily ahead. She wore a long djellaba (a traditional North African loose-fitting hooded robe) that flowed like wizard's cape, the hem dancing around her leather slippers. Mom's usually strong Fire seemed to disappear, and she went into the pressing worry of Earth, her secondary element. She and I were braced to not trust anybody and kept our gaze to the stones below our feet. But Maddie smiled, waved, and never looked back. Her Fire was burning brightly.

Maddie was a soft (yin) Fire. Nonetheless, she was still a Fire, and her flame was charming everyone in her path. She became everybody's long-lost friend. As soon as a wandering minstrel or vegetable vendor started to lure us into his colorful tent, Maddie would turn to us, say something delightful in Arabic, and the entire corner of the souk would fall in love with her and get us out of the vendor's grasp. Where did Maddie learn Arabic? And how was she hypnotizing these skilled vendors who were trying to persuade us to buy everything from olives to gold? The guidebooks warned us not to giggle or smile, but Maddie was doing both!

Moreover, she was in total control. Trays of mint tea miraculously appeared everywhere she went. Prices came down and treats were offered as Maddie laughed, conversed, joked, and charmed even the snake charmers. Old men were melting over her. Women who'd looked as if they'd like to slit our throats were now radiating joy. As if she had a magic wand, she made everyone in the souk swoon for her. Maddie melted all of Marrakech.

Fires are lit from the inside, and they are the life of the party. They are everybody's friend, and they're often the ones with lampshades on their heads trying to make everyone laugh. They are the ones who jump up on the dance floor first, the ones who crack jokes all night, and the ones asking the band to play just one more song, long after the other guests have left.

Fires are complex, but they don't lead with complex or complicated personalities. They are the bubbles on the surface of the champagne; they lead with love and passion. Fire people are fun, easygoing, and exciting, and they always win the popularity contests. They remind the rest of us that life really can be a celebration.

Fires are rarely embarrassed. Why would they be? Life is a grand experience, and there is nothing to be embarrassed about. A recent study reports that 50 percent of people are afraid they'll look stupid at the gym, learning how to use the equipment and wearing workout clothes. I believe that the other 50 percent of people in that study were Fires (although I can't confirm this, of course)! The Fire is the man strutting through the gym in pink tights, blue shorts, a bright orange headband, and a muscle T-shirt that says DO YOU THINK I'M SEXY? He doesn't care how he looks; he has his headphones on, and he's rockin' out, lifting a barbell here and rolling on a yoga ball there. It isn't so much that Fire types don't have a fashion sense, rather that they don't care what other people think. Life is to be enjoyed, and if pink tights and a bright orange headband are fun to wear, then why not?

Fires do well in many different types of jobs because they transform tasks and to-do lists into fun. If you have a Fire teacher, you'll be inspired to learn and want to go to class every day. A Fire waiter or waitress will have you laughing through your meal and will seem like your best friend serving your food. A Fire CEO will keep employee morale high, although not many CEOs are Fires, because they have too much fun in life to be bothered with fighting their way to the top.

107

As far as countries go, few have more Fire qualities than Australia (which also has Wood). It is difficult to see "typical" Australian culture because individual Australians are so creative. Instead of assimilating to someone else's style, which would create a culture for the whole country, individual Australians create their own. In general, they like to have a good time; they enjoy celebrations and parties, good humor, jokes, and wordplay.

In the 1986 movie *Crocodile Dundee,* Paul Hogan plays a crocodile hunter who is always happy, even when battling crocodiles, strangling snakes, or facing knife-wielding teenagers in New York City. He has no malice and is often telling jokes, no matter what the situation. The Fire attitude is very simple and very positive.

Fires Exude Charisma

Fires are consummate performers. They love to be seen on television or the big screen. Recall Tom Cruise's explosive Fire energy when he jumped on Oprah Winfrey's couch in 2008 to show the whole world he was in love (being in love is a Fire feeling). He could barely contain himself!

Gene Kelly was a dancer, singer, and actor who transformed the image of the male dancer from balletic, supple, airy, and smooth to athletic, strong, energetic, and vivacious. He used tap dancing to express joy and exuberance. One of his most famous roles was the lead in *Singin' in the Rain*, a movie that some regard as the best dance film ever made.

Directors loved to work with Kelly because he was not afraid of ridiculing himself. He loved poking fun at himself. He was extremely disciplined (Wood) and also highly energetic (Fire). Debbie Reynolds, who was eighteen when she starred in *Singin' in the Rain*, said it was hard to keep up with Kelly, who was forty. During the famous scene when Kelly twirled his umbrella joyously, splashing and dancing in puddles, he was running a temperature of 103°. Inspired by the way children play in the rain, his Fire energy pulled him through his sickness.

Before he was famous in movies, Gene Kelly was a camp counselor. Entertaining children is a perfect job for a Fire. Later he organized Beverly Hills parties in his home—another excellent example of a Fire in his element. Watch clips of Gene Kelly whenever you feel blue, and you will feel better.

Fires love inspiring joy in people. Actor Robin Williams, who had a lot of Fire (and also Water and Earth), said that one of his favorite things was to make people laugh. Ellen DeGeneres, another celebrity with a lot of Fire, says it's her job to make people happy. She is a master at transforming pain into comedy so it becomes entertaining. Rita Moreno, in the iconic movie *West Side Story*, displays her Fire (and Wood) with her explosive and sexy Latin energy in the role of Anita. Anita is saucy and confident, with an expansive voice and dramatic gestures that make her character very exciting. Janis Joplin, considered the First Woman of rock 'n' roll, was a Fire (and also a Water) whose performances were described as electric.

Performers who are not predominantly Fire often find a way to pull up some Fire whenever they're in a public spotlight, because they're fully aware that fans are drawn to happy, energetic celebrities. Behind closed doors, however, they may need to return to other elements to restore themselves.

109

Uncomfortable at Parties? Go with a Fire!

Alex was a well-known sommelier in the Napa wine region of California, and being with him was always a fun adventure. When he invited me to the big Domain Chandon champagne party at the company's sprawling winery, I jumped at the chance and drove up from Southern California. Most of the two hundred VIPs had driven up from San Francisco and were lounging around the terra-cotta patios and picnic tables, relishing the beautiful rolling hills, the warm summer breeze, and the live band, flown in from Portland, Oregon.

Lots of swanky young people made the event sexy and entertaining. Alex made friends with all of them. He easily melted every cliquish group, offering good laughs and invigorating chitchat about grapes, wine, champagne, and life. Spending a few minutes here and a few minutes there, within forty-five minutes, we had met everyone at the event, and Alex was everybody's best friend. The men liked him, the women liked him—everybody loved Alex.

I was having the time of my life, but before long Alex was bored. He wanted to explore the vast acreage of the estate. The event was held in a small section of the winery, but Alex wanted to go where we weren't supposed to go—beyond the signs that said, NO TRESPASSING. TRESPASSERS WILL BE ARRESTED. As I hesitated, Alex climbed over the large chain and strolled ahead of me down the vine paths, with a bottle of wine in hand. As a sommelier, Alex was always carrying a bottle of the finest wine. I followed him down the dirt path. He stopped to touch some grapes along the way, but mostly he walked freely with a smile on his face and a glow of freedom in his eyes. I tried to keep up. I scanned the area constantly for anyone who might be watching us and wanting to shoot us.

Just as Alex was finding a spot to sit and open his bottle of wine, a loud voice came across the land. It was from a beefy security guard with a bullhorn, standing on lookout from an upper balcony of the Domain Chandon building. "Stop right there! Both of you! Turn around! Walk toward the building!" I don't like breaking rules and I don't like to get caught breaking them. I was embarrassed and ashamed.

But not Alex. For him, it was just another adventure in the present moment. With a huge smile, he called out, "We got a little lost! We're so happy you found us so you could guide us out! Hey, I have a bottle of vintage Bordeaux—drink it with us! We're coming up!"

Not only did Alex render the security guard speechless, but we found our way out and Alex made a beeline for the top of the building. Once we got there, Alex greeted the security guard like an old friend, promptly opened the wine, and asked the guard if he could find us some glasses. The guard left and returned a few minutes later with glasses and even a basket of warm bread. We all laughed, told stories, and held our glasses up to toast the golden sunset of a California afternoon.

Fires Enjoy Life and Want You to Enjoy It Too!

Fire people give to others in hopes of making friendships and connections. They are cheerleaders; they want others to be happy. They feel good (and more worthy) when they have brought others into the light. But they won't sit and listen to your sorrows as an Earth will. Instead, they'll think of distractions, things the two of you can do together to avoid the darkness in your mind. A

111

movie! A dance! A bar! The beach! A couple of jokes! Ice cream! They will throw lots of fun ideas your way until they see a glimmer of hope. If this cheering succeeds, not only will you feel loved, but the Fire person will have a dopamine rush too. Everyone will be happy!

At thirty-three, I was a successful Middle Eastern dancer who had been performing at resorts and events in Egypt, Lebanon, Tunisia, Jordan, Greece, Turkey, Dubai, and all over Europe for several years. Then I decided to return home for a time. In Southern California, I performed at weddings and Middle Eastern restaurants that catered to dignitaries and local business people of Middle Eastern origin. I prided myself on being professional, skilled, seasoned, reliable, and one of the best in the business.

Middle Eastern nightclubs in California were a kaleidoscope of music, laughter, dancing, families, and friends. Some families that frequented the clubs had been watching me perform for more than a decade. I enjoyed a reputation as a top dancer and was invited to many private homes to perform at parties, bar and bat mitzvahs, birthdays, and anniversaries.

My shows at the restaurants usually started around midnight. When I finished, I would leave the venue promptly and drive to my next gig or go home. I never stayed to dance with the customers, never accepted drinks, and never partied, even though the scene lasted for many hours after my performances. I wanted to be considered a person who took my art seriously, not someone who danced because it was a fun hobby, as many amateur belly dancers did.

I wanted the world to know I was a different kind of dancer. I was classically trained. I took everything seriously, from the dance training to learning about the various cultures, their history and music, and the people who had birthed these dances. I knew part of my "superstar" reputation was built on having a mystique and not getting too close to the crowds. I constantly monitored myself: How I entered or exited a restaurant was important; it mattered to whom I spoke. Since I was my own manager, it was important for me to set rules for myself and follow them (a very Wood trait).

One night another dancer, who was a Fire, caught me backstage after my show. She asked me to stay and have fun. We could dance the night away, she said. I told her no and gave her a long list of reasons.

"Come on!" she said with a twinkle in her eye. "You're thirty-*free*! Not only are you at the top of your game, but you're in the prime of your life. You'll never be this age again with all of these people loving you and supporting you. Everyone out there came to see your show, and everyone out there wants to dance with you."

She told me to let go and have fun. What good would it do to simply leave the club as I always had? She asked me if my rules were allowing me to enjoy life. Did I really want to go home every night after my shows while everyone else danced to live music and enjoyed their friends?

Based on her Fire wisdom, I started staying in the clubs after my shows. I allowed people to buy me delicious Lebanese meals and pour me expensive champagne. Most of all, I did what I really wanted to do—I kept dancing long after my own shows were over. I found terrific dance partners, made friends who had previously just been faces in the crowd, and had one of the best years of my life. I was finally able to let go of my strict adherence to professionalism and experience the joy that I hadn't allowed in my life. It took a Fire to remind me that having fun didn't mean I was unprofessional.

113

Fires Are Impulsive

Fires often lose themselves in others or in the *now*, especially if the environment is very stimulating (something Fires love). It is not their nature to analyze, so in the heat of the moment they don't always have discernment—even about their own opinions. Fires are quick to respond to people, bouncing off others' energies, following what feels good, and completely losing themselves in the give-and-take. They can have trouble staying focused. If a lively conversation or interaction feels good, they go with it. But later they often discover what they truly feel is quite different. Because of this, they may seem untrustworthy or fickle; then the changeability boomerangs back to hurt them—and also others if they don't understand this about Fires.

The Arabic nightclub scene in Southern California before 9/11 was fun and lively. Wealthy Middle Easterners, Mexicans, Israelis, Europeans, and Americans would fill the venues around 11 P.M., ready for the belly dance show at midnight backed by the best live Arabic bands from the Middle East. Everyone was dressed beautifully, champagne flowed, and the crowded restaurants were filled with smiling faces. After the show every night, people danced. Then the crowd migrated to someone's house to continue the party. I never attended the house parties because, after performing four or five shows a night within a hundred-mile radius all over Southern California, I was usually exhausted and ready to get out of my costume, melt into my couch, and watch the 3:00 A.M. episode of *Cops*.

One night, as I was leaving the restaurant with a girlfriend, a woman announced that the party would be moving over to her house. She asked me if I would come. I politely turned her down. She then invited my friend, who excitedly accepted. We left the restaurant and I told my friend to have fun at the party. She told me she had no intention of going. What? I was confused. She had just told the woman inside that she was headed over, and several people had heard her. She said she was thrilled to be asked to join the party and knew she would have a ball. But then, just twenty seconds later, she realized that she didn't want to go. Such is the capricious nature of a Fire.

Talking with a Fire can feel like a racquetball game. On the court the ball is moving fast and bouncing everywhere—into the corners, up high, down low, behind and in front of the players. The players have to be ready to hit that ball. There is no resting—it's a game of total interaction. And it's fun! But sometimes you look back on the game and think, *Wow, she was all over the court. She hit me with the ball, and now it hurts a little.* Did she do it intentionally? Probably not. However, it can still sting, especially for a more careful element type.

Fires often interrupt conversations and can leave a trail of hurt feelings without even meaning to. Their lack of discernment can be a wonderful quality, though, because their love isn't censored or limited and neither are their words. You don't get a bunch of filtered, canned conversation with Fires; you get what they're feeling in the moment. However, it can also be a roller coaster, and they can be quite inappropriate, especially when they don't feel they're connecting with someone or if there's silence. They will try to fill in the gaps with conversation, nervous laughter, or endless talking. This often happens at events that are already strained, like funerals and church services. They may try to warm up the crowd with meaningless chatter or even jokes, which don't always go over so well. The good news is that you can tell Fires about their missteps, and they will probably hear you and be able to move on, instead of creating a heavy issue from the feedback. More than any other element, Fires bounce back.

Befriending a Fire can be a golden opportunity to see the magic and humor in life, to rise out of your doldrums, and taste some of their infectious joy and pleasure. But if you aren't uplifted by their presence, they might not stick around. They want to let go and dream big when they're with you, to be in the receptive mode of desire. They want to *enjoy* you. If they can't, they may look elsewhere.

Fires and Emotion: Panic

While most elements have two governing organs or parts of the body that have impact on them, according to traditional Chinese medicine, Fires have four: the heart, the pericardium, the triple warmer, and the small intestine. The pericardium is the sac that protects the heart. The triple warmer is a system in the body that regulates the fight, flight, or freeze response and is the mastermind of the immune system. The small intestine does most of the digesting of the foods you eat and emotions you feel.

Fires have huge hearts and embrace everyone. They love feeling love and inspiring happiness in others around them, so it makes sense that one of their governing organs is the heart, but when that heart energy is out of balance, Fires often panic. They can panic over seemingly small issues that don't worry any of the other personality types at all. For instance, Fires can become very panicked about what is happening in their workplace, the challenges facing their children, troubles with finances, and a myriad of other things in life. Sweaty palms, a rapid or irregular heartbeat, fluctuating blood pressure, and illogical thinking are all signs of panic. They start to imagine the worst-case scenario, and they have a difficult time seeing the bigger picture of what might happen next, tomorrow, or in a year. Because they are so completely in the moment, it is difficult for them to remember that there are phases in life and that just because something looks doomed in this moment doesn't mean that it is.

Imbalanced Fires may suffer from insomnia, anxiety, and an unsettling feeling of internal chaos. In extreme cases, sustained panic can affect the health of their physical heart too, so it's important for Fires to stay calm, even when they feel like running around yelling, "The sky is falling! The sky is falling!" Help a Fire keep on an even keel by gently touching their arm or back and speaking in a normal (but not condescending) tone about what is happening. Fires' imaginations tend to run wild, so stick to the basic facts. Help them draw a clear picture. Their panic may seem dramatic and unrealistic to you, but to them it is very real. Instead of telling them that there is no reason to be upset (which they won't hear or believe), reassure the Fire that all will be OK. Don't try to restrain Fires by telling them to calm down or not overreact, because this will make them panic more and then resent you when they do calm down.

Remember, in Chinese medicine, the organs are directly connected to the emotions. The energy of the small intestine is said to quiet the mind and not allow distractions to overwhelm the heart. The small intestine protects the heart by removing physical waste and also by releasing emotional baggage that would otherwise be overwhelming. It is very important to keep the small intestine as healthy as the heart through healthy eating, energy medicine, and acupuncture or acupressure. Fires need to be mindful of too much stress. It's easy for them to feel bombarded. They need to slow down, clear their schedules, and declutter their lives.

If a Fire in your life is panicking, he or she may resemble a caged animal ready to lash out. Traditional Chinese medicine says that if the heart does not remain calm, connection to the spirits is lost. Western studies show that people who panic are more vulnerable to heart attacks, strokes, and heart disease. You will be doing a Fire a huge service if you can help her or him to come back to a comfortable and positive place.

DO!

Do stay aware that you are a great influence on others. Just by being someone who enjoys life, you're a role model. This can be transformative for others, who don't always feel the same joy and jubilation that you do.

DON'T!

Don't let your imagination run away with you. Instead, take inventory of what's actually happening to avoid overreacting and letting your nervous system go into fight, flight, or freeze mode. Learn techniques for avoiding panic, and use them often.

Even the Energizer Bunny Needs a Break

Jenny was called the Energizer Bunny. She owned her own successful dance studio in Los Angeles, which catered to celebrity performers. She traveled around the world as a professional dancer with more than twenty-five over-seas contracts a year and she had a strong and stable relationship with her husband back home at a beautiful house in Malibu.

Jenny's schedule was packed from dawn to dusk. She rose at six A.M. for morning meditation, followed by a dance class. Then she would teach a dance class, take a yoga class, work out with a professional trainer, and cho-reograph dances for her two international dance companies. In the evening, she would make dinner and spend time with her family, watching a movie.

Her schedule didn't stop there. She also kept up with social media and had a successful monthly e-letter. She housed dancers from around the world in her home as part of her traveling dance ensemble. She spent time in recording studios helping to orchestrate all-original music for her cutting-edge dance shows. And she was friends with all her neighbors.

Jenny could be a real taskmaster (Wood), but because she was so strong in Fire, she could still be joyful and humorous without becoming dictatorial for too long. She took business seriously but never so seriously as to not enjoy life. She soaked up every bit of pleasure and fun she could and went along her jour-ney with a positive attitude and passionate dedication. She laughed often, smiled a lot, and chose activities and opportunities that brought her happiness and passion.

However, every once in a while, Jenny would crash. The stress would hit her when she least expected it, and she would become anxious. Her enthusiasm would dim. Usually, she was an entertaining talker, but when she was crash-ing, she would sound confused, exaggerated, and melodramatic. Her sen-tences would sound disjointed or disconnected. Apathy would set in, as well as emotional flatness. It was difficult to regroup. Life seemed to lose its purpose.

Physically, Jenny would suffer insomnia, dizziness, and fatigue. She had to fight to get her energy and drive back. Over time she would always nurse herself back to health with lots of rest and start all over again with as much energy as before, if not more.

I worked with Jenny for years and was envious of her ability to let go of the past difficult moments and move on. Even if her shows received poor reviews, her dancers were fighting, or travel visas weren't being issued, she never took any of it so personally that it was a roadblock. She could let go of the past and move on—one of the more enviable traits of a Fire personality and one the rest of us can all learn from.

Fires get overwhelmed after expending a lot of energy over a long time. Burned out, they suffer panic and emotional chaos. They want to get out of their own skin because it has become so uncomfortable. They are like a large, hollow, lightning-blasted tree, with fire still burning inside and quietly smoldering on the ground around them.

To get back on track, a Fire can work with the heart energy and utilize calming techniques throughout the day, like brief interludes of mindful meditation; even a few moments of stretching helps the heart to calm. Ultimately, Fires realize that they probably can't do everything they want to do in the time they want to do it in, and they will need to not schedule themselves so feverishly. With the extra time in their schedule, they may be able to incorporate power naps, and extra hours of sleep at night, which make a Fire person healthier and more dynamic in the long run.

Fires and the Body

Many Fire-dominant types are slim, athletic, or fit-looking because they burn a lot of energy. They have a bounce when they walk and seem to dance down the street. They are very light on their feet. They can become distracted by an attractive person, a city statue, or an amazing lake and suddenly veer off to see whatever caught their eye.

A lot of Fires have curly, frizzy, or flyaway hair like fire flames around their head. Their clothing can be anything from spandex workout clothes to lots of bling, layers, and colors—whatever brings them joy.

Movement for Fires

Fires excel at high-energy exercise like Zumba, bicycling, jogging, skiing, team sports, and fast couples' dances like the jitterbug. Fires don't usually have patience for sitting on a yoga mat, walking slowly on the beach, or leisurely swaying to music. Often, though, this is precisely what Fires need to come back from spreading their energy far and wide. It can be balancing for Fires to take on slower, more calming movements like swimming and Qigong.

Moreover, Fires usually have a faster metabolism than other elements. They are able to burn off calories easier than most people, and strong Fires seem able to eat whatever they want. However, most Fires need cooling foods in order to balance themselves mentally, emotionally, and physically. Some of the main cooling foods are milk, ghee, butter, avocados, cilantro, mint, unrefined olive oil, and unrefined coconut oil. Foods that have a heating effect should be

121

avoided, such as cayenne, chilies, curries, and alcohol, which can tax the digestive system and affect the heart rate.

On the other hand, iced drinks are often not good for a Fire. Fires are ruled by the small intestine, an organ that works hard to digest food and absorb nutrients. To do this, it needs to stay warm. Digestive organs work like the boiler room on a ship. Situated deep in a lower compartment, the boiler room contains heat-generating equipment to make sure the ship runs well. Drinking ice water is like throwing water onto the boiler's flames, making it work harder to maintain its heat and run the ship. With ice-cold drinks, your small intestine has to work much harder to keep your digestive system in optimum working order. A drink without ice is assimilated into your body faster because it doesn't disrupt the system.

Supporting your heart and small intestine with healthy foods and drinks doesn't have to be a chore. Nuts and seeds are very good for the small intestine, as well as fermented foods like kefir, sauerkraut, and yogurt, which contain vital probiotics.

Because more people die of heart disease in the United States than of anything else, it's easy to find information online about heart-healthy foods. Omega-3 fatty acids, for example, are well known to support the heart. They can be found in the three superstars of heart-healthy foods: sardines, mackerel, and wild caught salmon.

Fires are not governed just by the heart, pericardium, triple warmer, and small intestine, but also by several other parts of the body, like the circulatory system and the adrenals. Fires are often more prone to adrenal burnout than other elements because the adrenals are affected by overstimulation, and high stress, especially in high-strung or nervous individuals (even if they're nervous only when they panic).

Adrenal burnout has been called the stress disease of the twenty-first century. The adrenals are two walnut-size glands that sit on top of the kidneys and help control blood sugar levels, the balance of salt and water, and the stress response. If you are often stressed, physically or emotionally, the adrenals get tired and don't work as well. This adrenal fatigue can show itself as dizziness, an inability to cope with stress, and low stamina. Certain foods can help heal your adrenal glands—those rich in B vitamins, vitamin C, and the amino acid l-tyrosine.

Many Fires are also sensitive to electromagnetic pollution. Cell phones, microwave towers, television sets, microwave ovens, and computers all give off strong electromagnetic fields. The World Health Organization reports that low-frequency electromagnetic fields induce circulating currents within the human body. Though further research on EMFs is needed, reported symptoms include nausea, loss of libido, fatigue, headaches, dizziness, dehydration, depression, and suicide. EMFs have electrical properties and Fire people are more susceptible to EMFs than other elements.

YOUR HEART LOVES THESE HERBS

- Green tea
- Oregano
- Garlic
- Ginger
- Turmeric

YOUR SMALL INTESTINE LOVES THESE FOODS

- Apples
- Carrots
- Raspberries
- Asparagus

Eden Energy Medicine Exercise for Fires: Triple Warmer Smoothie

A meridian is a pathway of energy on the body. The triple warmer meridian governs the emergency response to threat—fight, flight, or freeze. It is the human thermostat, involved in regulating the endocrine system, the autonomic nervous system, and appetite. The triple warmer smoothie sedates the triple warmer meridian and helps to restore peace and calm. It also helps regulate body temperature, hot flashes, and panic—to all of which a Fire is susceptible.

124

1. Place the pads of your fingers on your temples.
2. Take a deep breath in through your nose and out through your mouth.

3. On another deep in-breath, slowly slide your fingers up and over your ears.
4. On the out-breath, take them around and behind your ears, down your neck, and hang your fingers on your shoulders.
5. When you are ready, push your fingers into your shoulders, drag them across the front of your shoulders, and let them land on your heart crossed over each other. You can do this as many times a day as you would like. It is an inconspicuous exercise that you can do at work and at meetings, and you will probably find that you love it because it will make you feel calm and grounded.

Finding Balance as a Fire

Randy worked for the cruise lines, traveled for a living, and met lots of different people, freely sharing the warmth and passion that bubbled up from inside him. His days were filled with activity, and his nights were opportunities for celebration. On his days off, he would sample local cuisine, go parasailing, kayaking, or mountain climbing. When the day was done, Randy almost always persuaded someone to share a nightcap at a local watering hole.

But some nights Randy couldn't find anyone to indulge him. His mood would swing from upbeat to disappointed. Unable to sustain the feelings of euphoria from the day, he'd become jittery, restless, and insecure. He would question his sense of value. As Randy's joy turned to panic, he would rush around trying to please everyone, even strangers in a bar, ordering drinks for them while talking nervously. His heart would beat rapidly and his conversation would be full of needless statements. After a while, he'd become withdrawn and apathetic. Randy's high energy started pushing people away when what he really wanted was connection. He became resentful of people who didn't want to hang out with him and be in his social bubble.

Randy underestimated the power of turning in early, tuning in to himself, and replenishing, which are crucial for a Fire. Fires crave the company of people, and pleasure with others will always lure them, but they finally need to take a shower, go for a swim, be in nature alone, write, or just read a book so the dizzy feeling of being unloved and utterly exhausted can pass.

If Fires can't find moments of calm and relaxation, their attention may jump all over the place, and they'll have trouble staying focused. They're not great at remembering things in the first place (because they don't hold on to the past—at all), but when stressed or unable to connect with others, they will barely remember what happened that same day.

When Fires can't find people to join in their adventures and can't get the social connection they crave, shifting their awareness can be a great gift they give to themselves. A massage can move the lymphatic fluid, promote relaxation, and open the heart. Along with massage, relocating the Fires' focus with Bach flower remedies, rest (without talking), and sound and light therapy are all good ways to balance an overactive mind.

Most of the time, Fires are magnets and will have a very big social life. When I first experienced my friend Holly, she drove me nuts. I was a serious Wood actress and we would end up on the same film sets in Florida. I found her loud, obnoxious, way too happy, and all-around annoying. But my being irritated by Holly didn't bother Holly at all. She pushed through my resistance to become my friend. Soon after, I fell in love with who she was. She loved life!

Holly had a huge social circle and threw the best parties. She was connected with everyone who was anyone in show business: casting directors, producers, writers, actors, and makeup artists. She was on a mission to throw the greatest industry parties in the history of South Florida and to make sure everyone had fun. She would bop from conversation to conversation, noting which hors d'oeuvres were being passed and ensuring that the champagne was being poured. Everyone loved Holly and everyone loved her food. She had a ball cooking and designing trays of colorful, fun, interesting platters. She rolled her own sushi, mashed her own potatoes, and kneaded her own dough for pizza and flatbread. Then there were the desserts! Holly spared no colors, textures, or decorations with her tailored cupcakes and mini macaroons with individual names of all the party guests and a little trinket hanging off of each tiny treat. There was food in the microwave, food in the oven, food all over the kitchen! The party began and Holly kept emerging from around the corner with more food, more drinks, more fun, and more joy!

As a Fire, she almost never fit in everything she wanted to do, though she always thought she could and would panic when the clock was ticking down. She would run around like a chicken with no head, picking up random objects and putting them down, feeling extremely pressured even though the pressure was self-imposed. She spoke four languages but suddenly couldn't string a clear sentence together from any of them, and many times she would become hysterical. This momentary Fire explosion would cause her to run around like a madwoman doing everything but nothing at all, because now she couldn't keep it all together. Panicked thoughts about how she wasn't going to make it

127

would cause her to explode even more as guests U-turned away from the kitchen and quickly retreated to the back rooms so she could have her space. Her energy ran high; she had an unforgettable laugh, a loud voice, huge gestures, and facial expressions that emphasized everything she said, thought, and felt. She wore the latest fashions with the reddest lipstick and a giant smile, and you could always hear her saying, "Oh my God, you have to try this! You *must* try this! Try this, and this and this and this—you will *love* it!"

EXERCISE TO BALANCE FIRES
- Swimming
- Slow dancing
- Yoga

BALANCE YOUR HEART, PERICARDIUM, SMALL INTESTINE, AND TRIPLE WARMER
- Acupuncture
- Acupressure
- Eden Energy Medicine

CALM YOUR FIRE
- Stop
- Gently breathe
- Step outside to scream, stomp, and cry. Allow the calm to come.

Fires in Relationship

My friend Sebastian was in town and wanted to meet for a drink. When I arrived at the bar, he crossed the room with super speed and was suddenly by my side. He whipped me up into a giant hug and spun me. "Sweetheart! How are you?!" he bellowed.

Sebastian didn't wait for my answer. Instead, he introduced me to the restaurant staff and several patrons. In the twenty minutes he'd waited for me, he had met everyone. We talked about work, family, friends, and everything in between, with cocktail waitresses coming by frequently to flirt with Sebastian, who already knew their names. Before long, he asked if I wanted to have sex back at his hotel. When I said no and reminded him that I was in a committed relationship, it was no big deal, as though I had said no to an extra olive in my martini. "No worries," he quipped. "Just thought I'd ask!"

I hadn't seen Sebastian in years, so I asked him about being married and getting divorced, but instead of telling me about his ex-wife or his daughter, he told me about cooking at his own wedding. There had been 250 guests, and it was highly stressful—a dumb idea, he concluded. But he also described each dish, down to the amount of spices and which exotic vegetables he'd used.

Wanting to hear more about his family, I asked him about his daily life.

"Life?" he answered. "Life! What is life but an opportunity to love everyone! Everyone wants love and I am here to give it! Life is too short not to love, love, love!" OK, Sebastian. He seemed not to have changed since college.

Being in a relationship with a Fire can be both exciting and frustrating. Fires yearn for intimacy, but they get bored and need variety. They are prone to overcommitting to people because they go where the energy feels good.

They will jump from person to person just like a raging wildfire that jumps freeways and races up mountains. Fires are drawn to pleasure and fun, so they often abandon people or events that lack excitement, passion, and romance. They are loyal and dedicated until something doesn't feel good. Then they move on to the next pleasurable experience. This may mean that they end up being serial monogamists or "best friends" with many different people. Therefore, it can seem as though Fires love everybody and that their love for an individual isn't so special or sincere. Perpetually in motion, Fires are always distracted by the next shiny object.

In romantic relationships, Fires want sparks to fly; they don't want the honeymoon to end. Many Fire couples have excitement and embers burning bright, for years. But if you aren't a Fire or you can't access your Fire, it can be very difficult for your Fire partner. This is especially true for Waters, who like to drop deep into their cave and not be swinging from the chandeliers.

One of the worst things for Fires is to feel that they need to subdue themselves for the sake of others. When Fires feel inspiration (which is often), they need to go with it, otherwise they are put off their rhythm, a discontent that can be very painful in a relationship.

The passion, joy, and electricity that a Fire embodies and craves may seem shallow, ephemeral, or unreal. But do not mistake their heat, passion, happiness, high energy, and bright light for a phase. This is the foundation of a Fire's being and these things are as real as fear for a Water, anger for a Wood, compassion for an Earth, and grief for a Metal.

In relationships with Fires, being clear about your boundaries can help them keep theirs. Being clear about what you want and need in the relationship will help keep them on task with more forethought in their decisions instead of being swept up in the river of the moment. However, making sure there is enough variety in the relationship also does wonders for Fires' equilibrium.

For people who don't live in the energy of a Fire, it can be very difficult to comprehend what living in the present moment is like. Fires not only live in the present moment, but they also feel at home in it and experience it as a realm of joy, pleasure, and happiness. Like Earths, they cannot bear to see people suffer, struggle, or get left out in life, so they say yes a lot but often realize later that maybe they should've said no.

For people like my mom, who are a strong combination of both Fire and Earth, it is unbearable to witness someone hurting emotionally. She describes her reaction as a physical pain that feels like a heart attack, and she will instinctively do whatever it takes to reduce that person's suffering. This can be very difficult for Metal and Wood, who can be very sympathetic but don't have that same chord of pain that triggers them when someone is hurting. A Metal or Wood doesn't always understand this need of Fires and Earths to make other people happy or fix other people's pain. A Metal or a Wood may mistake this for a Fire or Earth wanting people to love them.

The enemy of Fires is sameness. They don't expect you to be perfect, but they do expect you to keep showing the love and excitement they evoke from you. One of the best ways to do this is through open communication. Avoid letting the relationship lapse into stagnancy with lack of communication. They want to feel that you care. They may frantically try to get you to talk to them; if that happens, talk to them! Give them what they need! Why not? If you do, you may be blessed with one of the most fun and exciting relationships you have ever had.

Jimmy Buffett—a Laid-back Fire

In 2002, I was hired to dance for Jimmy Buffett's fifty-sixth birthday. I had little idea of what to expect. I just knew that I was a surprise and I would dance for him backstage at his concert.

I was not a follower of Jimmy Buffett, so when we pulled into his sold-out concert at Irvine Meadows, California, I was surprised that the entire parking lot had been turned into a beach. Thousands of people had brought their own sand, beach umbrellas, beach balls, tiki torches, inflatable swimming pools, palm trees, coconut bikinis, inflatable sharks, and pot. Lots of it. None of the police or security guards seemed to care—everyone was there for the love of one man and his music. However, Jimmy Buffett isn't just about the music; there is a Jimmy Buffett lifestyle, and he has thousands of fans throughout the world called Parrotheads. It is said that you will gain more friends at a Jimmy Buffett concert than anywhere else in the world.

I was escorted backstage and was told that I could enjoy his concert from the VIP seats until I was called. I understood immediately why people loved him. He exuded joy, laughter, good vibes, and humor. He often poked fun at himself and would interrupt his own songs with laughter and jokes. He dressed casually and in bright colors. He never stopped smiling and seemed to make everyone's world a happier place. His vibe was all Fire. There was nothing too serious in his lyrics and nothing too serious in his commentary. He just wanted people to have a good time and forget their daily grind for a few hours.

When the moment came, I was taken backstage. Jimmy's band members had brought him back and blindfolded him, put him in a chair, and started my music. I danced in, the blindfold came off, and he was delighted and surprised to see a belly dancer. I danced around him, with him, and for him. He was happy and carefree. When I motioned for him to copy me, he did, and he had fun shaking his shoulders and hips. I put his hands on my hips, bumped him out of his chair, and put a beautiful shimmering gold and black turban on his head. He celebrated every move I made and relished the surprise and the pleasure of the performance.

Suddenly, he had to go back onstage. I watched from the wings as he sang to the crowd of thousands in my turban. My turban! He was still wearing my turban! I had to get it back. It was my favorite turban, plus my Wood was loud and clear in my head, "It was MY turban!" For the next hour, I tried to get my turban from a very adamant and angry costume designer who said they would be keeping it. She said that Jimmy liked the turban and it was now his. With some stern orders on my part, between songs a stagehand pulled the turban off Jimmy's head and reached out to hand it back to me—but the costume designer insisted on sketching it first so Jimmy could have his very own.

Do You Know a Fire?

Fires aren't difficult to recognize. They laugh out loud and often continue laughing when everyone else is done. For them, life is a party and living it is a ball!

You will probably smile, shake your head, and want to get up and dance when you think of the Fires in your life, past or present. There is an uplifting, lively rhythm to their existence, and they seem to not get stuck in the muck that slows down the rest of us.

133

The feeling of being with a Fire is the feeling of being in love. It's a wonderful thing that many people search for all their lives. If you can access your Fire or if you have a Fire in your life—as a friend, lover, spouse, or family member—this will be the gift that Fire brings, that feeling of being excited about all of life.

Fires have the natural ability to pull other elements out of stubbornness, darkness, depression, boredom, and worry into the land of the living. Their energy, laughter, and high spirits are contagious. Spirit, warmth, and enthusiasm will transcend your ordinary existence when you are with them. Get ready to go out, because they're headed to their next event!

Remember, if your partner is a Fire, he or she wants to feel adored and beautiful. While other elements might feel flattery is insincere, Fires love it and will melt when they know you are paying attention to them.

You May Be a Fire If . . .

You may be a Fire if you try to cram everything into one day and you never have enough time to do it all or see all the people you want to see. Does joy immediately propel you into clarity and inner calm? Do you feel optimistic when you wake up in the morning—ready to live life and take every moment as it comes? Are you someone who needs to be around others to bring you back to your center? Are you a person who understands pain but feels there is enough joy to not have to dwell on the pain? If you are smiling to yourself, laughing, and nodding, then you are most likely a Fire.

134

IF YOU THINK YOU ARE A FIRE . . .

○ Remember that most people don't have as much energy as you. They may have a hard time keeping up. It doesn't mean they're sick or injured or that anything is wrong with them.

○ When you're jumping from one topic to another and getting all your thoughts into a conversation, you may be interrupting others. You may think you're sharing, but they probably think you're steamrolling them.

○ Be aware that people are attracted to your spirited joy, and they may think you are much closer to them than you really are.

○ You are a natural salesperson, but don't take advantage of people just because they believe everything you say.

○ If you are flitting from one committed relationship to another, whether short-term or one-week stands, your partners (and friends and family) likely won't view that behavior as commitment.

○ Wait before you say yes. Think about it. Sleep on it. Have a meal. Wait.

○ You can go through the daily grind with high energy for a long time, but you can't go forever, and your body might suffer if you try. Take a break. Come back to yourself.

○ When you're feeling anxious and panicky, the situation probably isn't as bad as it feels. Ask a Wood for a realistic report.

○ If you're in a bad mood and you haven't eaten in several hours because you're on the go, the cause may be hypoglycemia. Eat.

135

Fire Personality Assessment Quiz

Take the following quiz to find out how strong you are in the Fire element. Chances are that you're a combination of elements. This means some of these answers will be true for you and some won't. The quiz results will tell you how dominant your Fire characteristics are within you. Accepting, understanding, and working with the elements that compose your personality are crucial to understanding the actions and motivations of others and being at peace with yourself.

Rate the following statements according to your tendencies. On the scale of 1 to 5, 1 is never true and 5 is always true. When you are finished, add up your scores and compare them with your scores for the other elements. A high score may mean that you have found your primary element. You are led by your primary element (or shared primary elements), which will dominantly reveal those respective traits in your personality, but you will be very influenced by your secondary, and to a lesser degree, the third, fourth, and fifth elements. In certain circumstances you may draw on elements as a coping mechanism or strategy, but they may not be heavily present in your day-to-day life like your primary element(s).

1	2	3	4	5
Never True	Almost Never True	Sometimes	Almost Always True	Always True

Are You a Fire?

UNDER STRESS I EXPERIENCE THE FOLLOWING:

_____ Panic

_____ Dehydration

_____ Confusion

_____ Scatteredness

_____ Perspiration

_____ Nervousness

_____ Anxiety

_____ Insecurity

_____ Hypersensitivity

IN GENERAL:

_____ I love sharing food.

_____ I am intuitive.

_____ I love a good story—even if it isn't true.

_____ I can talk people into whatever I believe in.

_____ I feel joy and I express it through the way I move and speak.

_____ I express unconditional love.

_____ I usually feel very warm toward others.

_____ I like people and I want to be around them.

_____ I am enthusiastic about life and whatever is happening.

_____ Pleasure has a stronger pull than getting my work done.

_____ I am emotionally responsive to people.

_____ I love physical contact and I initiate it.

_____ Loud music usually doesn't bother me; it just makes me want to move and dance.

_____ I am comfortable being the center of attention.

_____ I choose stimulating environments in which to travel and play.

_____ Being onstage or in the limelight really energizes me.

_____ It is easy for me to share my positive feelings.

_____ I love talking about what I love.

_____ I am often the life of the party.

_____ I like living in this moment right now and I celebrate it!

_____ I laugh and giggle without inhibition.

_____ I see humor in all aspects of life.

_____ I thoroughly enjoy receiving.

_____ I never take things too personally.

_____ I tend to talk loudly and laugh loudly.

_____ When I meet people, it is easy for me to be intimate with them.

_____ If people are angry, I can melt them and make them forget why they were angry.

I love having high expectations, even if things don't work out well in the end.

I am upbeat and optimistic, even when things don't look so good.

I absolutely love celebrations, holidays, and gatherings.

Feeling panic is very familiar.

I avoid negativity and I make light of difficult situations.

I am spontaneous, optimistic, and energetic.

I am prone to exaggeration.

I am empathetic.

I never analyze enthusiasm.

My heart is broken one moment and fixed the next.

When I sit, it isn't for long. I like moving.

I walk or dance with a lot of zeal—skipping, bouncing, and lots of funky dance moves!

I like high-energy exercise—Zumba, aerobics, and running!

I speak with enthusiasm and can sound as though I'm laughing or smiling through my words.

TYPICAL PROBLEMS FOR FIRES:

My attention can jump all over the place; I have trouble staying focused.

I can become hysterical when overwhelmed.

139

_____ I can get nervous exhaustion from spreading myself out to too many people.

_____ I can get very scattered and become completely disorganized.

_____ I can work myself into a frenzy.

_____ I panic when others lose energy, and I furiously stoke their fire.

_____ Under stress, my words can become chaotic and sound like gibberish.

_____ I get bored with slow events and slow people.

_____ I sometimes cannot separate my own thoughts and feelings from those of another person.

_____ I am sometimes in love with more than one person.

_____ I compulsively live for parties and celebrations.

_____ I can be addicted to love, sex, and spirituality.

_____ I panic when there's an unexpected demand on me; it can confuse me.

_____ I feel I am much too accommodating to what the other person wants in a relationship.

_____ I have a very hard time saying no.

_____ **SCORE FOR FIRE**

CHAPTER 4

The Earth Personality
Bringing People Together

*When we practice loving kindness and compassion,
we are the first ones to profit.*

—RUMI

EARTH ARCHETYPES:
  The Mommy ▶ The Preschool Teacher ▶ The Caretaker

THE SEASON:
  Equinoxes and solstices (transition)

STRESS RESPONSE:
  Worry and enable

FAMOUS PEOPLE WITH EARTH ELEMENT:
  Pope Francis
  Mister Rogers
  Dolly Parton
  Ed Sheeran
  Disney's Snow White

IF EARTH PEOPLE WERE ANIMALS:
  The Golden Retriever
  (lovable, loyal, friendly, kind)

POPE FRANCIS

Earths are like a cup of hot cocoa and a warm fireplace or a homemade berry pie on a summer evening. They love comfort, and they love to comfort others. They are surrounded by friends and love to spend time cuddling their kids and grandkids and cooking scrumptious meals for their families. Whatever allows them to feel that they can be themselves and give to others is where they want to be.

Earths hold the space of calm during transitions. Think of the solstices and the equinoxes, the times between the seasons. Earths embody this "time between"—the ability to flow and not be rushed. Because they understand transitions and also because they're good listeners, Earths are often caught in the middle during difficulties between people, and they have a need to honor "both sides of the story." Unfortunately, they also have a lack of assertiveness, partly because they never want to embarrass anyone, including themselves. Hence, they can appear wishy-washy and ambivalent.

Earth people make everyone feel loved. They accept others for who they are, welcoming their vulnerabilities without judgment. They truly believe that love is all we need to make this crazy world spin. They are the adored grammar school teacher, the caring mom who never yells or speaks in a "tone," and the caretaker who makes everyone feel special, spending extra time with people long after the caretaking work is done. Earths care about people, and they want everyone to feel like a VIP.

Earths are very good workers. They aren't workaholics, like many Woods, but more like good little worker bees. As an employee, they are excellent collaborators and personal assistants. They want you to be able to relax and trust that they will get the job done and done well. They take pride in being dependable.

Earths pour their devotion into their relationships. If you are friends with an Earth, you have probably received something made with their hands—homemade bread, a pie, some chicken soup, or a hand-stitched quilt. Their nurturing nature comes from deep within the heart and shows itself through generosity. They quilt, sew, garden, cook, or paint so they can give handmade gifts to others, and they often have a difficult time charging people for their merchandise or services if they are self-employed (which many Earths are), because it's hard for them to work in big companies and corporations. The exchange of money can be uncomfortable for them.

It is not as easy to find strong Earths in the history books, as it is to find other strong elements. Schools and history books today still feature curriculum in which students learn about people who fight battles, soldiers who forge ahead, countries that dominate, dictators who shock, and political figures who enforce policy and rule powerful nations. History books tend to focus on conquest and cruelty, not empathy, and Earths are the ultimate empathetic people—plus, they're too altruistic to want to be memorialized. The Earth type of people who heal the wounded, save the environment, sacrifice for others, serve the masses, and persevere with peace-based projects just don't get as much limelight. After all, it's not often that you hear about Iceland, Austria, and Denmark making the news, which, according to the Institute for Economics and Peace, are the most peaceful countries in the world. History and news feature the strong Wood countries, and also the strong Wood people who govern those countries, as well as the controversial Fires who set the world ablaze, the deep-thinking Waters who give us philosophy, and the spirit-seeking Metals who sit on mountaintops and gain notoriety by aligning with political leaders for world peace. However, if you look at the teachers, nurses,

143

and caregivers of our world, most are strong in the Earth element—OK, maybe not Nurse Ratched from Ken Kesey's novel *One Flew Over the Cuckoo's Nest*, but most of the other nurses are.

The World's Handsomest Earth

I was looking into the eyes of one of the most mesmerizing men in the world, spinning and swirling with my diaphanous veils while he smiled and clapped to the rhythm of the drums. He seemed to reach into my soul and touch my heart with his large, deep-set, smiling eyes. Omar Sharif was a legend, and I had been hired to perform for his sixtieth birthday on a small island near Miami.

I was twenty-three years old, and even though *Doctor Zhivago* and *Lawrence of Arabia* were movie hits before my time, I was fully aware of Omar Sharif and the magnetic power of this dark, handsome man who epitomized the term *movie star.*

From the moment I made my entrance at the pool area of the large estate and laid eyes on him, I could tell that he exuded the kinesthetic warmth of an Earth element. Every gesture supported me as a performer, and he embraced me with his attentiveness. He was fully present and giving me his all as an audience member.

I had chosen my music carefully, opening with an Egyptian classic from 1957 called "Tamra Henna," meaning "Lotus Flower." Omar was obviously pleased as he tapped his feet and swayed to the music. My second song was "Miserlu," and again Omar seemed happy with my choices and rose from his chair to dance with me. I was in heaven, dancing with Omar Sharif and hypnotized by his happiness and generous spirit as we held each other's hands over our heads, laughed, and shared the beauty of Middle Eastern dance, which means so much to Egyptian culture.

As my third song started, within seconds I knew it was not a good choice. But in 1992, my career in the Middle East wouldn't start for another six years, and minding cultural taboos of Middle East relations had not yet become second nature to me. I had always been friends with both Jews and Arabs and I didn't understand the faux pas I was making by choosing an Israeli singer to honor an Arab.

The artist I chose for my third song was Ofra Haza, a singer of Yemeni descent. Her music was a glorious celebration of love, life, and people. It had an Arabic flavor and rhythm and was popular throughout the Middle East. But she was Israeli.

As my song started and Hebrew singing came through the speakers, Omar's eyes widened. He slowed in his dancing and said to me softly and plaintively, "Is this Israeli music?"

I smiled enthusiastically and said, "Yes!"

He gently smiled back and said he couldn't dance with me anymore. He sat down.

The faux pas that I had made hit me in an instant and I responded with concern on my face about the confused look on Omar Sharif's face. He encouraged me to keep dancing. He sat at the edge of my stage, watched me intently, smiled, clapped, and continued to be the best audience member I had ever had, despite my making one of the worst cultural mistakes that one could make. Even though I triggered feelings of confusion for him and he couldn't

145

join me in the dance, he supported me one hundred percent, without embarrassing or shaming me—just as an Earth element would.

After my performance, I was escorted to a large suite near the top of a winding marble staircase. I wasn't sure what I was doing in the suite. Champagne, caviar, and a bounty of food lay before me on a long glass table. Was I supposed to eat it? Was I supposed to change into my regular clothes? I sat on the edge of a giant brocade-and-silk-covered canopy bed and waited. I figured that, at some point, my driver would come to get me, or the security guard would tell me I could eat.

Fifteen minutes later, the door opened. Like the grand entrance of a movie star in his big scene, Omar Sharif walked in.

Oh my God! I got it! Omar Sharif was coming to bed the belly dancer! *No, no, no—that is not what I wanted. What would I say? What should I do?* I decided to let him speak, and I would listen. My knees were already weakening and my heart was beating out of my chest.

Omar said he wanted to check on me and make sure I was well-fed. He asked me what my favorite food was and I told him it was shrimp. He thanked me for making his sixtieth birthday a happy one. He told me I was "such a good dancer" and prepared me for something he needed to tell me.

Here it was—the pivotal moment. I knew he was either going to berate me for dancing to Ofra Haza, the Israeli, or he was going to tell me that he would now get what he wanted—sex.

To my surprise, it was neither. He sat down on the bed with me, held my face in his hands, and told me that I was too young to be belly dancing. In an incredibly sexy accent, he slowly kept repeating, "You're just a baby." He then told me that I needed to eat and that I was too thin. (By American standards, I was considered full-figured.) He asked me several times if I needed anything before he left the room. A couple of minutes later, a silver platter of giant shrimp showed up.

Omar Sharif oozed kindness and gentleness. I felt that I was in the presence of a deeply caring father figure. It didn't matter that I had done something that could have caused my dismissal from the grand affair; Omar was a compassionate, understanding man who didn't let cultural differences spoil the event. He embodied the very best of the Earth element, a deeply sensitive thoughtfulness for other human beings.

Here are a few notable people who are or were strong in the Earth element. Mary Breckinridge introduced midwifery to America and wanted to bring health care to all rural poor families in America. She accepted little or no money for her services and traveled by horseback to deliver babies and provide family care to people in the Appalachians of eastern Kentucky.

Walt Whitman (who also had a lot of Water) opposed slavery and volunteered as a nurse during the Civil War. It is estimated that he visited, read to, and ran errands for eighty to a hundred thousand wounded, sick, and dying soldiers. He was also employed as a schoolteacher but refused to punish by paddling, involved his students in creative games, and joined them in playing baseball and cards.

Esther Kalenzi is a modern-day Earth (and probably Wood, which is a very balanced combination) who has a smile that can light up the world. In 2012 she decided she wanted to realize a long-held dream of helping children in need. She opened a page on Facebook and asked all of her friends to donate anything they could during Lent. She then asked them to join her on Easter weekend to deliver items to kids at two different orphanages and to celebrate, play, and dance with the children. From this beginning, Esther created a charity organization to help children everywhere, called 40 Days Over 40 Smiles.

Ben & Jerry's is an example of an Earth organization. Ben & Jerry's was started in Vermont in 1978 by two childhood friends, Ben Cohen and Jerry Greenfield. Early on, they began giving a percentage of their profits to fund community-oriented projects. They have joined in cooperative campaigns for children's needs, farms, the environment, action on global warming, Occupy Wall Street, and against oil drilling in Alaska. For many years, Ben & Jerry's had a policy that no employee's rate of pay should exceed five times that of entry-level employees. Today the starting pay at Ben & Jerry's is higher than the minimum wage (usually double the minimum wage). The company helps the unemployed get jobs, community service is a part of its mission statement, and the corporate offices in Vermont are dog friendly. The company is an advocate for humane, high-quality treatment of cows; fair-trade sourcing of ingredients; and for marriage equality, and all Ben & Jerry's employees can take three pints of ice cream home with them every single day!

Earths Need to Give to Themselves First, or It Probably Won't Happen

Even though Earths dole out lots of compassion to others, many of them have a hard time feeling compassion for themselves. They can become stubborn about not needing help. If they ask for help, they feel they're putting someone out or being a burden. Their mission is to help others, not the other way around, so they often suspend their own needs and desires. Earths often feel, deep down, that giving to another is more important than being nurtured themselves.

Robin Williams—a Fire for the Media, an Earth Behind Closed Doors

As I was writing the Fire chapter of this book and thinking of celebrities and their elements, Robin Williams immediately came to mind. I spoke to a friend of mine who knew Robin well and spent several years in friendship with him before his death. I told her I would like to write about Robin and include him in my Fire chapter. She said, "Oh, but his Earth was just as strong as his Fire." My friend recalled many times when Robin would have her and their social circle of friends in stitches. She said they would take drives through Napa, California, near Robin's home, and she would be laughing the entire time. It is true that he had a lot of Fire, but there was also a side of Robin that was very Earth, a side that the public didn't see as much.

My friend regaled me with stories about Robin's steadfast love for his children, his immense generosity to anyone with whom he came in contact, his devotion to people, and his tenderness of heart.

It's well known that Robin helped actor Jessica Chastain with a full ride to Juilliard, his alma mater, when she was starting her career; he gave Juilliard scholarships to several others as well. Robin's rider is another testament to his character. A rider is a list of an artist's specific personal and technical needs to do a show—anything from a private jet to pick them up to a specific type of wine in the green room to lighting and stage requirements. Robin's rider in-

149

cluded a requirement that for every single event or film he did, the company hiring him also had to hire a certain number of homeless people and put them to work.

In typically compassionate Earth fashion, Robin loved animals—especially dogs. But most of all, he genuinely loved people, a love for all humanity that is one of the most endearing qualities of an Earth.

If Earths can give as much love to themselves as they give to others, their lives will have more balance and harmony. To have happier and more productive lives, they need to separate themselves from the outcome of helping others. A partner or friend can help them to choose themselves first and give to themselves first. Supporting them to avoid being overly compassionate, overly giving, and overly present for others will help them with emotional balance.

Earths Love Relationships

For Earths, life is about people. Connections, friends, and love are very important. Earth people almost always have children. But in the rare cases when they don't have kids, they will pour their love into caring for animals or teaching children. Earths are hoping to bring the world together, so animals, kids, and adults are all friends. They want people everywhere to be loving neighbors, to visit, tell stories, and sing songs. They are like Mister Rogers, who sang "Won't You Be My Neighbor?"

Earths go with the flow; they support the team, and they stay after school with their students. Teaching elementary school is the perfect job for the Earth person, because with young children, the love is pure and the conflicts are still fairly simple. Usually a sticker, a cookie, or a gold star will fix any issues.

As far as countries go, there are few "Earthier" countries than Fiji. Fiji is a group of more than three hundred islands in the South Pacific, and Fijians have been called the friendliest people on earth. They are generous and loving, and their hospitality has no limits. Fijians will gladly invite you into their homes and allow you to stay as a guest while feeding you home-cooked meals and giving you whatever they have, which usually isn't much. Many Fijians are poor, but you would never know it—their happiness and joy abound. They are truly rich in spirit. Many Fijians live off the land, eating fruits from the thick jungles and feasting on wild pig, or fish cooked in the ground. They resonate with the earth, the oceans, flowers, trees, plants, and animals. They appreciate the world and their part in it. They represent the Earth element at its finest.

Earth people reach out to others and want people to know that they don't have to carry burdens by themselves. Earths are about community and building a solid infrastructure in which people can feel loved and safe. Burning Man, an annual gathering of tens of thousands of people in Black Rock City, Nevada, is a very Earth event. The ten guidelines for the event, drawn up in 2004 by the original founders, reflect the best of Earth. They include radical inclusion (everyone is welcome), gifting (the event is devoted to acts of unconditional gift giving), radical self-expression (honoring each person's unique gifts), and communal effort (creative cooperation and collaboration).

|51|

Princess Di—the People's Princess

Diana Spencer, who married Charles, the Prince of Wales, in 1981, has been called the People's Princess because she was so accessible, caring, and nurturing to commoners. From the beginning, Princess Di seemed to shuck the cold and proper mannerisms of royalty, preferring a more down-to-earth and warm-hearted representation of the British royal family. She was celebrated for her extensive charity work and often visited people in hospitals. She said, "I spend time with patients, holding their hands and talking to them. Some of them will live and some will die, but they all need to be loved. I try to be there for them."

Princess Diana was a magical mix of Earth and Metal, and many of her Earth traits came through in her care for human beings. As a teenager, she received an award for outstanding community spirit. She always had great interest in children, working in a kindergarten and as a nanny before marrying into the royal family and having two boys of her own, Harry and William. Even Diana's sharpest critics agreed that she was a devoted, dedicated, creative, expressive, and affectionate mother.

Diana exuded compassion for all people and was open about her personal problems, like depression and bulimia. She wasn't above us. She wasn't afraid to expose her problems, especially when trying to help others. This is what an Earth will do to create understanding among human beings.

Earths have no problem mustering the energy to take care of others. They work hard to bring people together, to help them connect and love each other. Earths always give attention to the lowliest: the people who need help, are lagging behind, or need more time than others. When a person is ready to throw their hands in the air and give up, it's the Earth person who'll be there to assure them that everything will be OK.

Over the years, a few movies have portrayed Earth elements in characters such as the demure and feminine Hadass in *Yentl*, and the sweet and idealistic Dorothy in *The Wizard of Oz*. But almost no character embodies the Earth element more accurately than Melanie Hamilton in the 1939 classic *Gone with the Wind* (based on the 1936 novel by Margaret Mitchell), about our war-torn United States during the Civil War. Melanie, the sister-in-law of Scarlett O'Hara, is kind, thoughtful, and charitable. She is affectionate toward Scarlett, even though her sister-in-law is a bratty, arrogant young woman. She volunteers at an Atlanta hospital. Melanie is the solid foundation of her social circle and seems to have no prejudice, unlike many other women of her time and place.

At one point in the movie, Melanie finds herself having a very meaningful discussion with Belle Watling, the town prostitute. Belle says to Melanie, "I'm scared somebody will recognize this carriage if I stay here any longer. That wouldn't do you no good. And if you ever see me on the street, you don't have to speak to me—I'll understand."

Melanie's response to Belle demonstrates the most beautiful Earth nature: "I shall be proud to speak to you, proud to be under obligation to you. I hope we meet again."

In another scene, Melanie takes her wedding ring off her hand to give to the war effort, even though her husband may never return from battle, and she does it with truth, honesty, love, and generosity in her heart. There are no ulterior motives—simply a heart of gold.

153

Earths don't like struggle, and they don't want to see anyone struggling or suffering. They are the first ones who will ask, "How can I help? How can I be of service to you?" They want people to feel grounded, stable, connected, receptive, and peaceful, and they will try to harness those feelings in those they love. Sometimes their need to bring others to contentment verges on excess and is alarming to people of other elements. My sister feels guilty every time she says no to a single male stranger asking to be her friend on Facebook. Men from all over the world—India, Indonesia, the Americas—used to get e-mails from her telling them why she couldn't be their Facebook friend instead of simply declining them with one click. She is finally weaned of that habit but not without thinking long and hard about their feelings. As a Wood, this type of thing has taken me a long time to understand about Earths. It pains them to exclude people, and I often have to remind myself of that.

Earths Are Drawn to People in Need

Jim was a big, burly, round man with an infectious smile and sparkling eyes. Everyone loved him. He lived with his family in a small mountain town in Virginia, and everyone in town leaned on him. Need a truck to move some heavy boxes? Jim was there. Need someone to help shovel the snow away from your front door? Jim would do it. He loved his two adult daughters equally and was a present and supportive father.

Mandy was considered the responsible daughter. She moved out at eighteen, went to college, had a consistent job managing a spa, and never asked for money as her sister did. When both Mandy and her sister Lisa had children, her dad gave more money for school clothes, toys, and gifts to Mandy's sister. Lisa expected (and received) Jim's financial support.

Intellectually Mandy understood her dad's deep desire to help her sister, who always seemed to be in need, even as an adult. But emotionally, it wore on Mandy all of her life. Sadness and resentment crept in. She felt it wasn't fair for her dad to help her sister, who was less responsible and less together. Plus, by the time she was an adult, her sister relied on Jim's cycle of handouts to get by. She never became responsible—she didn't need to grow up. Jim was always there.

Likewise, the inequality caused a rift in Mandy's relationship with her dad. Mandy felt less loved, less acknowledged, and less noticed than her sister. But Jim's Earthy heart would leap out of his chest to those who needed it most, even if it caused dysfunction elsewhere. He didn't notice the imbalance his giving caused; he noticed only the people who were struggling and the fact that he could help them. He suffered for those in need, and the need always seemed urgent. As with most Earths, Jim would do anything to help.

Earths Love Unconditionally but Need Reciprocation

Earths' need to give to others is so strong that they often look for something to give even if it's inappropriate or the gift is over the top. The interaction can become very imbalanced. For instance, when people are nice to my mom—who is a combination of Earth and Fire—whether be it a store clerk or a waiter, she immediately starts looking for something to give them. She rummages through her purse, looks in her car, or will even run into a store to buy some-

155

thing for the person—anything to show her appreciation. It can be very awkward. Sometimes I have to talk her out of her need to give because it doesn't make sense to the other person.

Earths are eager to be helpful and are earnest in wanting to make people feel valued and included. It pains an Earth to see people excluded or feeling excluded, and a strong Earth remembers all the times when he or she wasn't there for someone. But the truth is that, even for generous Earths, out-of-balance giving can go on for only so long, and the obligation they feel to people can become heavy. When imbalanced, Earths can also have an extreme need to be needed, which can be a huge turnoff to others. (This characteristic may sound a bit like a Fire, but an imbalanced Fire instead needs camaraderie and social fanfare from *groups* of people.)

My sister Titanya is a fantastic dance teacher and a strong Earth (she also has Fire and Water). She is warm, caring, accepting, nurturing, and fun. The students in her classes feel loved and cherished. She lets them borrow her costumes, use her dance props, and take lessons for free if they don't have the money to pay in any given week. She will also happily accept a donation. She used to have a little donation basket at the classroom door, and it was often filled with feathers, oranges, shiny rocks, and love notes. For a while she had a sign that said, LOVE DONATIONS. Some of her students thought they were donations from her to them, so they would actually take them for themselves! She no longer uses that sign.

One year, when she was living in Colorado, I spent a weekend as a guest teacher in her classes. I charged an amount that valued my time and was fair for the students. I taught, put my money in the bank, and that was that. My sister lamented that she rarely was paid on time and had been letting people take her classes even though they didn't have the money. She became more upset as she thought about the rental fee of the studio, the preparation in compiling music, and the time it took to put together the choreographies, all which she loved to give but was becoming less interested in giving away for free.

At my sister's house, her costume closet, which was usually overflowing with costumes, was almost empty. There was a lonely veil dangling from a hanger and an old coin top on the floor, but the big, bountiful costumes that she had made, bought, and collected over the years were missing. Where were her skirts and shawls, her chiffon and velvet masterpieces? She told me she had lent them all out to students. Some wanted them for Halloween and others just wanted to fantasize and dance for their husbands. At first, lending costumes out to her students was fun. She was excited to say yes when they shyly asked if they might borrow something. She loved knowing that she was playing a part in their happiness and their development as women.

As can happen with many Earths, however, my sister started to feel resentment that her generosity was not well reciprocated. Sometimes the students would keep her costumes longer than originally arranged; sometimes there were pieces missing when returned. Rarely did someone offer to return the favor. And even though she knew how to say no, she never was completely comfortable with that word, especially if it meant that someone would be disappointed or wouldn't feel as loved.

Earths and Emotion: Worry

Of all of the elements, Earths are the most resistant to change. Earths are governed by the stomach and the spleen. The stomach helps digest food and drink, and the spleen recycles worn-out red blood cells, stores blood for emergencies, and contributes to the immune system by producing lymphocytes. However, in traditional Chinese medicine, not only food must be digested and assimilated, but also emotions. Earths are all about contentment and peacefulness, so digesting emotions isn't always easy for them. Anything that's not harmonious won't sit well in the stomach. They ponder and ruminate decisions and feelings, unable to let them go and move on. Someone's feelings might be hurt! Someone might be left out! Think of the way cows "unswallow" and then rechew their food—they chew the cud! This chewing and rechewing is often what Earth people do with emotions.

Worry is a major emotion for Earths. Worrisome thoughts go around and around in their heads and keep them from accomplishing all that they would like to do. Earths who try to lead a project, company, or business meeting are in danger of getting stuck in these obsessive tendencies. A business meeting can easily turn into an unproductive series of indecisions. Earths may have to be comforted to come back to a place of ease, even if that means passing around a tray of cookies. This same type of worrying and ruminating can lead to over-mothering. As long as Earths are too wrapped up in the feelings of others, they will lose track of their own desires, becoming too involved in other people's lives and ultimately becoming intrusive or dysfunctional. When this happens between a mom and her children, it can prevent the children from learning by experience, being productive and resourceful, and ultimately adapting to life's inevitable changes. Instead of learning to see the bigger picture, smothered children can stagnate, lack direction, and get stuck in details, unable to find their way to clarity on their own. An unhealthy codependency is born. This codependency can follow Earths throughout their adult lives if they don't learn effective techniques to deal with their anxiety for others. Not worrying feels counterintuitive and even unloving to Earths, but they need to learn that they are not responsible for other people's happiness, their feelings, or how their lives turn out. Earths need to learn about emotional boundaries and separation between their lives and other people's. An Earth can practice compassionate listening, which can be incredibly helpful for the other person, and help the Earth not to lose herself in the process.

Earths' worry can also turn into guilt for not helping someone enough and not being there for them. Earths often overapologize, saying they're sorry for things that aren't their fault. They become self-sacrificing when this guilt sets in.

Emotions like worry can also disable other parts of an Earth's life besides their relationships. It's almost impossible for an Earth to travel light. They want to be prepared for every scenario—their own and others'—especially sickness or injury. That means they will have a kit of vitamins, Band-Aids, skin cream, aspirin, and Rescue Remedy. Of course, they always have extra food, mints, gum, and water. They often travel with a tea kettle, a small iron, a substantial sewing kit, and even a rice cooker. I know an Earth who always travels with her NutriBullet, a specialized blender. She packs enough clothes to stay twice as long as the trip, and back home she has enough food in the freezer for a zombie apocalypse. When she heads to the hotel pool for a swim, she has to do conscious breathing not to bring her purse and a small overnight bag, just in case!

159

My sister's Earth house and garden is like a museum and play area for people who want to bring out their inner child. She isn't exactly a hoarder, she says; she just loves stuff. She probably has more than two hundred elves, fairies, and gnomes around her home, which children love finding when they visit her. Her refrigerator is plastered with photos, and her kitchen counters are always covered with food—giant fruit and vegetable bowls, tubs of natural sweeteners, boxes of tea, bottles of vitamins and minerals, and food mixers of every type. If there is any space left over on a counter, some little gnome has made it his home. I've almost decapitated several fairies while trying to chop food. It's easy, with so many lit candles everywhere, to set things on fire in her house, with all the overhanging plants, cookbooks, and tiny collectible creatures everywhere.

My sisters' elves, fairies, and gnomes fulfill her childlike nature, her fantasy-loving creative side, and also her focus on children and things that children love. Her collection includes a giant pirate ship that she has had built in her backyard. Everything in her home is there because she resonates with it; she feels joy when she sees her knickknacks, collectibles, and tiny creatures. Also, she wants her guests to feel at home. My sister enjoys having guests and wants to accommodate every possible need that they might have. She tells stories to her guests about how she found every little fairy folk, what they remind her of, and the joy of discovering them and making them her own. She loves her things, and her things fill her house to make it a warm and loving home for people to feel safe and happy, including herself.

Earths' Homes Are Safe Havens for All

Maeve is the mother of one of my lifelong friends. She often sews me quilts and bakes me sweet cakes. She has become a sort of aunt to me, and when I was a teenager, I would often go to her little cottage after school. Whenever Maeve opened the door, sweet smells of baking wafted out toward me, and her sing-song voice melted all my cares away. Maeve's house was comforting, with lots of soft pillows, velvet chairs, lush curtains, photos, knickknacks, and keep-sakes cocooning the people who visited. She encouraged me to sit in a giant overstuffed chair in front of a crackling fireplace to show me the crafts she had been working on and feed me warm cookies. She always made sure I was well-fed. She had two or three extra-furry cats that roamed around her cottage; she spoke of them as her children. They were well-fed, loved, and cuddled too.

After a while, I noticed hundreds or thousands of trinkets lining Maeve's shelves and filling her antique armoires. Lace gloves from bygone eras, collections of tiny turtles, and fine china leaning on and lying atop other pieces of fine china. Then there was the bedroom. It was full of more pillows and a seemingly infinite number of stuffed animals. Maeve told me that some were from her childhood. She was saving others for the grandkids she was hoping to have one day. I had no idea how she even found her bed at night, because it was covered in teddy bears, dolls, and more stuffed animals of every color and size. If she never had grandkids, I thought to myself, her collections would be great to showcase at the county fair.

Earths have a hard time letting go of things and people. This is why they can find themselves in abusive or unhealthy relationships. They would rather stay in the familiar, even if that familiarity isn't physically or emotionally safe. For them, safety lies in the world they know, even if it's the predictability of an abusive partner. The world that they don't know (without the partner) is the scary part. This may sound unbelievable to someone like a Wood, who isn't scared of change, but Earths are very tied to the past. If they let go, change will happen. Of course, it becomes much more complicated and difficult if kids are involved.

In relationships, Earths want to smooth everything over and to soften any conflict. They believe that if they are kind and loving enough, they will bring the other person out of the darkness and into the light. But not addressing difficulties or differences keeps problems accumulating and, in the long run, creates more problems. Dealing with things is always healthier than trying to bury them. At the other extreme, however, imbalanced Earths can become so focused on their problems that they spiral into self-absorption and indecision. They can become so obsessed with what they should do that they do nothing at all.

When Earths can hear their own inner voice, they can be more concise and clear in their communications. They can love others and be peacemakers without losing themselves in a compulsive need to give. They can learn to midwife other people's transitions without becoming too attached to the desired outcome of a happy, fulfilled life for that person. They also learn to focus on their own transitions and to midwife those as well.

Balanced Earths find a way to redirect their thoughts and not obessively worry, often through connecting to planet Earth under their feet by taking a walk or spending time in nature.

162

DO!

- Do focus on what is needed now, not what will happen if there is change.
- Do create a plan with clear written notes to help you not worry about the unknown.

DON'T!

- Don't get lost in worry. Try to find the opportunities in change.
- Don't protect people from living their own lives. In the long run, doing so creates more problems.

Earths Take Care of the Earth

My grandma Edens was Earth and Metal. Her Earth side came out in many ways, especially with respect to the land, nature, and animals. On a trip to the Middle East with my grandpa in the 1970s, she collected sand and water samples in vials and brought them home for all of the grandkids to see (her Metal systematically labeled and found a perch in the house for each one). She loved trees and often knew the name of the ones lining the sidewalks and in the parks and woods. Grandma wanted each grandchild to know about geography, paying us $10 if we knew the locations and capitals of all fifty states. But one of the most Earth-inspired projects she did happened when the family went on trips. Grandma would take seeds in the car. Then all the way across America, Grandma would plant the seeds. At every potty stop, rest stop, or camping stop, she would teach

163

her three children about the seeds and the trees that would grow where they were planting them. As an Earth, Grandma needed to nurture the Earth.

Earths and the Body

Most Earth-dominant types are round, fleshy, and soft. This might not be true for the whole body, but you might see their Earth nature in their faces or tummies. They tend to hold on to weight, and when they walk, the extra weight adds to their swaying rhythm. Their walk is like a slow swish that seems to flow with every step. It is meandering, rather than a focused gait.

Earths prefer clothing that feels good. Plush velvet, flowing chiffon, silky tights, and soft cotton make them happy. Their hair and grooming is put together, but natural looking without a lot of extra products and chemicals.

Earths love food and tend to have a sweet tooth. Food is love! They gravitate to sweet treats, starches, and carbohydrates—potatoes, pies, breads, cakes, and pasta. They also tend to hoard food, especially when they aren't feeling loved. Treating every meal as though it might be their last, they often hide a private stash away, *just in case.* When I was little, I would plow through my Halloween candy–filled pillowcase in one week. My sister would still be pulling out bite-size pieces of Halloween candy after Thanksgiving, and I never did know where her secret stash was hidden. She would never dream of inhaling it as I did, because then there would be no candy left!

Earths often have an overabundance of food around and also tend to overeat. They are governed by the stomach, spleen, and digestive processes, so this isn't always good news for them.

The stomach secretes acid and enzymes to help digest food. The spleen filters the blood and fights certain bacteria. The stomach can be unsettled by too much sugar, carbs, or sweets. Likewise, deficient spleen energy can cause uncomfortable fluid retention in the feet, hands, and around the eyes.

Earths will overeat or indulge in unhealthy foods in an effort to fill themselves up with a substitute for unconditional love. But food will stop feeling like love once the digestive system complains.

A good way for an Earth to get healthy—other than to avoid overindulging—is to follow a gluten-free diet. Gluten is a protein naturally found in wheat, rye, and barley. Because so much wheat grown today is genetically modified, and because growing and harvesting methods focus on speed and quantity rather than quality, many people today have developed sensitivities to this protein. Once they eliminate gluten from their diets, many people lose weight, don't feel as depressed, see improvement in their skin tone, no longer have headaches, have more energy, and aren't as irritable. Physically and emotionally, they lighten up.

Earths with gastrointestinal issues may also want to try taking enzymes or probiotics to support digestion. These dietary supplements often alleviate stomachaches, bloating, gas, and even skin problems and canker sores, which are often caused by problems in the gut. There's lots of information about them online, and they are available at most health food stores. Some people have had such success with enzymes and probiotics that they take them every day.

Earths May Hold on to Weight, Even When They Diet

In the 1950s, my mom was required to take a home economics class. Home economics was a standard part of school curriculum in her eighth grade, designed to teach young people (especially girls) homemaking skills, such as sewing, cooking, cleaning, and caring for kids. One of the assignments was meant to show how calories work. The girls would ingest only a certain number of calories every single day for a week and record their food intake for confirmation. Based on prescribed calorie totals, the girls were told they would lose weight.

My mom recorded all of her calories, and the teacher calculated that she would lose six pounds by the end of the week. Mom was excited as she stepped on the scale at the end of the week, but to her horror—and this is unfortunately typical for Earths—she had gained three pounds. She learned later in life that Earths' bodies work very differently than the other elements' do. They often hold on to weight even when it should be melting away.

If the spleen isn't functioning properly or the stomach has digestive issues, weight gain and edema can result. Because Earths are governed by the spleen and the stomach, these physical issues can arise from the disturbance.

YOUR SPLEEN LOVES THESE FOODS
(The stomach is pickier about the specific foods your body will like.)
- Sweet potato
- Squash
- Black beans
- Fatty fish

YOUR SPLEEN LOVES THESE HERBS

(The stomach is pickier about the specific herbs your body will like.)

- Chamomile
- Alfalfa
- Burdock root

Movement for Earths

Earths do well with movement that is rhythmic and slow-to-moderately paced. They love music, and anything that feels "earthy" will probably feel good to an Earth—like Nia, a mind/body physical conditioning program (the initials stand for Non-Impact Aerobics). You don't find too many Earth types in the gym pumping iron or doing anything that requires a lot of regimented instruction. African dance, traditional belly dance, and partner dances, like swing, salsa, and tango are well suited for Earths, who also enjoy group dances, like square dance and line dancing.

Earths must find some kind of movement that they like to do and *can* do consistently. Like Waters, Earths avoid physical exercise whenever they can, preferring to lounge around talking and eating good food with friends. Like all elements, however, Earths need to exercise regularly. Finding fun movement to do with friends every week is the key!

167

Eden Energy Medicine Posture for Earths: Cross My Heart

This crossover pose of the arms calms the spleen energy and helps to bring restoration and love back to yourself. This exercise can also lift you out of indecision and worry. You can do this whenever you want to bring calm to your worried Earth mind.

1. While standing, sitting, or lying down, cross your arms and place your hands into your armpits. Place your thumbs straight up on your chest.

2. Inside your armpits, your fingers are wrapping around the spleen meridian, where they can help alleviate worry. The thumbs are on neurolymphatic points, which stimulate the flow of lymph in all organs. Your arms are crossing over the thymus gland in a posture that is excellent for the immune system. Your arms are also crossing over the heart chakra, a position that is excellent to help energies cross over the chest.

This posture is comforting to all elements, but it really helps Earths to come home to themselves and feel safe, thereby being able to adapt to change.

Finding Balance as an Earth

Cassandra lived in a wooded part of Oregon and could walk for miles enjoying the sounds of the animals scurrying, the leaves crunching, and the wind whispering through the trees. She walked rhythmically and slowly through the forest, singing softly. Her long brown curls floated over her shoulders, and her full, velvet skirt flowed around her legs. She didn't wear shoes. She loved walking barefoot in the grass, on the sand, in the leaves—anywhere that she could feel the earth under her feet. She often left her shoes at home.

She had three small boys and often nursed the baby as she walked. Singing to a suckling baby, walking through the forest barefoot, and being in touch with nature fed Cassandra and resonated with her own Earth personality. Being in nature always brought Cassandra back to balance. It especially soothed her if she'd had a hard day or an argument with her husband. But even if she'd had a day with no problems, walking barefoot on the earth brought her clarity and rejuvenation. It allowed her to feel more grounded, stronger, more alert, and always happier.

Earths can easily become overwhelmed. When this happens, they procrastinate, become indecisive, and have trouble with time. Doing things like walking in nature or doing something creative, like cooking or crafts, can help ease the stress. Deadlines, timelines, authority, rules, directions, and policies can

169

all be difficult for Earths, who prefer to live more fluidly. They need to take the time to create a comfortable atmosphere for themselves.

Always needing to take care of others and give their time to them, Earths can become stretched too thin. Even if intellectually they desire to take care of themselves, somehow that care often goes to others first.

EXERCISE TO BALANCE EARTHS
- Partner dancing
- Walking in nature
- Swimming

ENERGIZE YOUR EARTH
- Put on music and dance!
- Call or visit a friend.
- Cook, draw, paint . . . create!

BALANCE YOUR STOMACH AND SPLEEN
- Massage
- Acupressure
- Eden Energy Medicine

Earths in Relationship

Earths are usually great listeners and counselors to their friends. They will support everything that their loved ones do. They create the space for people to be their very best, to shine in a way that many people wouldn't be able to do without their support.

If you are in relationship with an Earth, let her help you. Even if you're a completely self-reliant Wood, find something with which the Earth can lend a hand. The need to give cannot be avoided for an Earth. Moreover, giving is linked to higher levels of oxytocin, the "happiness hormone." Let your Earth partner give to you, and your relationship will be happier.

Earths don't want people to feel bad or dislike them, so they are careful not to rock the boat. They will say what they think people want to hear and enable toxic relationships instead of challenging or leaving them. Change can be excruciating, so they hold on to the past, along with all of the people in it, no matter who they are or what they've done.

Peggy loved being married. She loved not working outside of the home; she truly enjoyed cooking and being a housewife. But a few years into the marriage, her husband turned violent. He would yell and throw things at her. Once in a while he grabbed her forcefully and screamed at her about nagging him, smothering him, and becoming too needy. Life became scary for Peggy, but the thought of leaving her husband was scarier. At least she could predict what would make him mad and when he would get violent. She couldn't predict anything that would happen if she left. He was the breadwinner, so if she left him, how would she make money? How would she find a place to live?

Peggy felt ashamed. She didn't want to tell her friends what was happening. Staying with friends would bring too many questions. And how would Peggy get a job without having a home? She decided it was better to be berated at home than to be out on the streets. Plus, Peggy still loved her husband. If she reported the violence, he could lose his job and be ostracized by the community—if people even believed her. She worried that people would think she was crazy or overreacting. After all, he didn't hit her.

Peggy coped by trying to keep her husband as happy as possible. She was raised to believe that it was her job to keep the relationship alive, and that if it failed, it was her fault. Every day she felt guilty. She blamed herself for the accusations and the belittling. If only she could be better.

Peggy believed her husband each time he said that he would never lose his temper again. After all, he was loving most of the time. When Peggy said her marriage vows, it was for life. She believed he felt the same way.

As the years went on, Peggy lost her self-esteem. She couldn't face making decisions anymore and was getting used to her life with a husband who took his anger out on her. She also began to doubt that she could ever find anyone better. Her husband constantly told her how good he was to her. They had a beautiful home; they went to nice dinners and took yearly vacations. Financially they were stable, and from the outside they seemed to have a perfect life. Peggy convinced herself that getting manhandled wasn't the worst thing that could happen—there were always worse things. She would say to herself, *The good thing is that he doesn't hit me.* Peggy stayed, even though her husband eventually cheated on her, for which Peggy apologized. She felt she owed her husband an apology for not being good enough for him to not cheat.

172

In her mind, this made sense. If she had been giving enough, had made him feel happy, and hadn't been so clingy, he wouldn't have cheated.

Earths can start to question their entire existence when they feel they don't please people, falling into codependent cycles that never seem to end. Even wallowing in regret or disappointment for years can seem safer than leaving and disappointing someone. Suffering can become comforting if it's familiar, and Earths will hold on to the familiar.

Most Earths deeply feel that they are caregivers and healers, and yet they have a hard time nurturing themselves. I asked an Earth friend what it's like to ask for help when she's in need. She responded by saying, "Ask for help? Are you out of your mind? I remind myself how good I feel when I help others and to let them have that same euphoric feeling of helping me that I get when I help people, but it's just an intellectual exercise. So I attract relationships in which I'm taking care of the other person. Then I wonder why *my* needs don't get met."

For as much love and understanding that Earths give to others, they need the same amount of alone time, creative time, and time for self-expression. They also need to learn to receive. Nurturing themselves will help them to build self-reliance and confidence. They need to practice hearing their own inner voices and truths as well as hearing the truths of everyone else in their lives.

Do You Know an Earth?

By now you probably know if you have an Earth in your life or whether you're an Earth yourself. When someone agrees with you about everything you say

173

and sees potential and value in all of your ideas, you'll know you have an Earth on your hands. Such people will give you their time, their heart, and their soul so you feel supported in life.

Earths love to be included, invited, and a part of events and projects. They want to be part of the team and the foundation that holds it together. However, they don't want to lead the team or be in the limelight. They enjoy the freedom to ebb and flow where needed, not where an authority figure tells them to be. They want to be the base that keeps the relationship stable, the glue that holds it together.

If you need someone to really listen to you, pay attention, and care about you, befriend an Earth. If you have Earths in your life, give them one of the things that they always give so well—compassionate listening. Although they rarely ask for help or company, because they don't want to seem needy, they do want to be seen, heard, and understood. Too often, they are overlooked because they don't come on strong with their opinions; they're soft and usually sweet. They also can be taken for granted as a bottomless pit of love and help. Therefore they're not always acknowledged. They may appear self-sufficient, but acknowledgement and understanding are often what they are really wanting deep inside.

You May Be an Earth If . . .

If you want everyone to be happy and you truly feel that love makes the world go round, you may be an Earth. Do you want to please others? Do you feel the need to make sure everyone is comfortable and comforted? Do you take time to connect with people and hear their stories and problems, even if it takes you away from your own work and projects? Are you a friend until the end who believes in forgiveness and making peace? Do you sometimes find yourself resenting people because you have given so much and aren't getting reciprocation? If you're reading this, softly smiling, and gently nodding your head, then you are most likely an Earth.

IF YOU THINK YOU ARE AN EARTH . . .

- You may worry too much for others, and they may feel smothered by you. Find healthy ways to vent your worries, so people aren't repelled by the heavy energy of your constant concern for them.
- Spend time with your friends. Don't pass this up because you don't have time or have a partner who doesn't want to go out and be around people.
- Be clear with people about your desires and goals, instead of just listening to theirs.
- Give freely without expecting love and understanding in return—and without resentment. Doing so will free you to trust and love yourself instead of relying on trust and love from others.
- You need time to make decisions. If people pressure you to "do it now," you might make a decision for them and not for you. You will regret it later and possibly resent them.
- You like to be fluid with your time, so use a gentle alarm and schedule system for yourself, so events and deadlines don't come upon you unexpectedly and put you into worry mode.

○ Some part of you will always suffer for others, but you need to find ways to detach from that suffering, or it will own your life.

○ If you say what you think others want to hear, it's likely that, in the end, no one will be as pleased as you had hoped, and you won't get your needs met.

○ Love does create miracles, but there are times when you can love people with all your might, and they still won't change or come to their senses. Let them have their path. You have yours.

○ Change can be positive and really fun. Find someone to help you navigate big changes and see them in a positive light.

Earth Personality Assessment Quiz

Take the following quiz to find out how strong you are in the Earth element. Chances are that you are a combination of elements. This means some of these answers will be true for you and some won't. The quiz results will tell you how dominant your Earth characteristics are within you. Accepting, understanding, and working with the elements that compose your personality are crucial to understanding the actions and motivations of others and being at peace with yourself.

Rate the following statements according to your tendencies. On a scale of 1 to 5, 1 is never true and 5 is always true. When you are finished, add up your scores and compare them with your scores for the other elements. A high score may mean that you have found your primary element. You are led by your primary element (or shared primary elements), which will dominantly reveal those respective traits in your personality, but you will be very influenced by your secondary, and to a lesser degree, the third, fourth, and fifth elements. In certain circumstances you may draw on elements as a coping mechanism or strategy, but they may not be heavily present in your day-to day-life like your primary element(s).

1	2	3	4	5
Never True	Almost Never True	Sometimes	Almost Always True	Always True

Are You an Earth?

UNDER STRESS I EXPERIENCE THE FOLLOWING:

_____ Worry

_____ Feeling of being overwhelmed

_____ Self-blame

_____ Indecisiveness

_____ Hopelessness

_____ Lack of focus

_____ Tendency to get very emotional

_____ Confusion

_____ Uncertainty

IN GENERAL:

_____ I love spending time with my family.

_____ I love having children and/or pets around.

_____ I love the idea of pregnancy, adoption, and being around moms-to-be.

_____ I truly want the very best for everyone and I will go out of my way to help them.

_____ I am glad to be relied upon for reassurance and help.

_____ I enjoy my social circle of activity. I love my friends.

_____ I like being the center of my family, a person the others can lean on for support.

_____ I want disputes to be settled and everyone to feel content.

_____ I accept all people unconditionally.

_____ I create comfort for everyone.

_____ I am accessible to my friends.

_____ I am very loyal and will be there for anyone in need.

_____ I am very diplomatic.

_____ I have great empathy for what others are going through.

_____ I give people the benefit of the doubt.

_____ Meeting and mingling with people I don't know is easy for me, and I enjoy it.

_____ If someone has an endearing quality, I immediately want to be around them.

_____ If someone is hurting, I often feel it is my responsibility to make her feel better.

_____ If someone feels left out, I often feel it is my responsibility to make him feel included.

_____ Everyone confides secrets and stories to me.

_____ Thoughts, feelings, and food seem interconnected.

_____ I serve others and help them in their transitions.

_____ I devote myself to people who love me even if I don't love them.

_____ I don't like change.

_____ I enjoy activities like cooking, gardening, homemaking, sewing, woodworking, and crafts.

_____ My home is very warm, and in it there is a comfortable place to sit for everyone.

_____ I would never humiliate or expose another person publicly.

_____ I support loved ones even when I don't agree with them.

_____ I get really comfortable by kicking off my shoes and snuggling in.

_____ When I walk, dance, or move, I often do it with a lyrical sway.

_____ I like exercise in which I can be with friends or a group of people in a noncompetitive atmosphere.

179

_____ I speak with a sweet tone that can resemble singing a lullaby.

_____ I don't want to take sides.

_____ Almost more than anything else, I want people to take care of each other.

_____ I squirrel away food just to be sure.

_____ I enjoy bringing food, gifts, or treats to parties and gatherings, especially if I make them myself.

_____ When people ask me questions, I feel obligated to answer, even if I'm uncomfortable doing so.

_____ I often find myself saying "I'm sorry" even if something isn't really my fault.

_____ I am not competitive.

_____ I sometimes wonder who will take care of me.

_____ I often give money or personal possessions to help people out of difficult situations.

TYPICAL PROBLEMS FOR EARTHS:

_____ I keep my problems to myself.

_____ I take on other people's burdens.

_____ I feel sluggish and defeated when I am overcommitted to people in need.

_____ I tend to overworry.

_____ I can smother people.

_____ I can meddle in other people's business.

_____ I am overprotective.

_____ I get overextended in my efforts to be a friend or counselor.

_____ I struggle with boundaries between business and friendship.

_____ I tend to collect stuff, or hoard, because things comfort me.

_____ Sugar and/or carbohydrates satisfy me like a heroin fix.

_____ I can get resentful after doing so much for people, even though it was my choice.

_____ I can feel sorry for myself if people aren't loving me enough or in the right way.

_____ I have a tendency to gain weight easily.

_____ I often keep the truth to myself if I think it will cause hurt feelings.

_____ **SCORE FOR EARTH**

CHAPTER 5

The Metal Personality
Yearning for Refinement

■

Grief is the price we pay for love.
—QUEEN ELIZABETH II

METAL ARCHETYPES:
The Queen ▸ The Ballerina ▸ The Yogi ▸ The Alchemist

THE SEASON:
Fall (letting go)

STRESS RESPONSE:
Detach and become aloof

FAMOUS PEOPLE WITH METAL ELEMENT:
Angelina Jolie
Barack Obama
Julia Child
Benedict Cumberbatch

IF METAL PEOPLE WERE ANIMALS:
The House Cat
(intelligent but often reluctant to be social)

ANGELINA JOLIE

Metals are like the Eiffel Tower in Paris, standing almost one thousand feet high and dwarfing the structures and landscape around it. Alone like a tall, bare tree at the end of autumn whose leaves are gently blown off by the early winds of winter. Their branches are bare, the limbs are long, and they reach toward the heavens, solitary in their quest. They are the ones letting go of what is no longer needed. Metals often lack companions, but as with the lone, tall tree, visitors come to sit with them. Think of the Buddha attaining enlightenment at the base of the sacred fig or banyan tree. When he sat at the tree he knew he was in the company of divine nature. Jesus Christ and Mother Theresa likely had a lot of Metal.

Like the season of autumn, Metals are about releasing, surrendering, and letting go of needless distractions, toxic thoughts, and unnecessary things. They are orderly and stoic, searching for a sort of perfection in life, a purity in all that they perceive and observe. They have high values and are usually very spiritual, often seeming more enlightened than the rest of us. They do not readily emote or discuss feelings. There is no space in the mind of a Metal to get anxious about the possibility of losing something, whether it is a job, a marriage, or a friendship. Their journey is to be one with change, not to hold on to something for dear life or melt into grief. Instead, Metals mindfully tend to keep their consciousness pure and their mind free of unnecessary thoughts.

Metal is the last in the Five Elements wheel (see page 244 for a visual). It represents endings. Subconsciously, Metals are letting go, releasing, and trying to finish up everything they were put on earth to do. They can have the energy of people in reflection or meditation who need to finish all their business before they attain nirvana.

The tricky part is that Metals' quests to free themselves from earthly possessions and reach higher consciousness often detach them from other human beings. The feelings, sadnesses, regrets, challenges, and emotions of others can become too heavy for a Metal. They often move away—physically and emotionally—from relationships that don't enhance their own journey, and they can seem indifferent or void of feelings and emotions when relating to people. Think of Spock from *Star Trek*. In the episode called "The Trouble with Tribbles," from the second season, Spock seems intrigued by the small, furry creatures called tribbles. His colleague, McCoy, says to him in surprise, "Don't tell me you've got a feeling!" Spock responds, "Don't be insulting, Doctor."

If Metals can learn to accept that other people's feelings are a part of life—that people get wounded, just as they also experience joy—then Metals will be more in touch with themselves and their own feelings, allowing them to connect with people more deeply. Allowing people to feel their feelings without judging them or detaching from them, even if it challenges Metals' comfort levels, may be one of the biggest heart openers that Metals can experience. Consistently opening the heart is important for a Metal, otherwise there can be a lack of flexibility in relationships.

Metals Are Cool and Collected

Hanna had wanted children from the time she was a young girl. Her own childhood was difficult. Her mother had been addicted to drugs, and her father figures never stayed around long. Hanna's mom often regretted having children, saying that life would have been much easier without them. Hanna never felt special or truly valued. She wanted to have children so she could make up for her mom's inability to nurture with love and appreciation.

By the time she was in her early twenties, Hanna had two sons. She raised them into responsible young men and autonomous adults. When her boys moved out and were living on their own, I visited Hanna. Hanna was active on Facebook, and I asked her why she never showed any family photos or photos of her sons. She said that her sons were their own people, not an appendage of her. She told me that she was quite proud that she had raised them to be expressive thinkers with individual minds who were strong in their own identities, separate from her and each other.

Hanna admitted that she was not a warm mom. She did not coddle her sons, take lots of photos, or even help them step-by-step through life. She had rarely hugged or held them as kids, and she didn't feel that physical contact was necessary for kids to know that they're loved and bonded to their parents. On occasion she told them she loved them, and she always sacrificed her own well-being to make sure they were fed, clothed, and safe—even when money was tight and bills weren't paid. She listed many ways in which she taught them honor, respect, and compassion for others. Their home was peaceful and companionable, and they always shared good times.

Hanna felt confident that she had raised her sons to be upstanding citizens with a strong sense of who they were. She felt she was a good mom, not because of how loving she appeared to be, but because she knew in her soul that she had raised them correctly and morally.

As a Metal mom, Hanna didn't need adoration, awards, or praise. She knew, from a higher place in herself, that she was a good parent. She was clear about the power dynamic between adults and children and was comfortable with the hierarchy inherent in these roles. She was also keenly aware of cause and effect. She treated parenting like a child-management program, with the goal of raising her kids, not necessarily to become best friends with her, but instead to be upstanding citizens of the world.

Metals are calm, cool, and collected. They do not get riled up, they do not engage in conflict, nor do they participate in drama. They like established plans with people and activities that will meet their high standards. However, very rarely does anyone meet Metals' high standards, including themselves. This can create a sense of disappointment that may add a layer of ashen silence to their already dry demeanor. Sorrow can be a subconscious backdrop of their life. Sorrow doesn't destroy or undermine Metals; it is simply a familiar companion and one of the many layers that make up their existence. A Metal's sorrow is not like a Water's sadness. Metals often continue with their work, play, and all of their normal activities while feeling a despondency that is well hidden under their already austere nature. Waters' sadness can't be missed—it is painful, gloomy, and dense, like a heavy fog.

Switzerland is a Metal country. It has the spartan demeanor of Metal: composed, pacifistic, and conflict-avoidant. Switzerland's popular saint, Nicholas of Flüe (1417–87) advised, "Don't get involved in other people's affairs." Switzerland has listened to these words and stayed out of other countries' wars. Instead, Switzerland has embraced one the greatest virtues of the Metal element: discovering solutions and transforming deeply rooted hostilities. Switzerland has done this by mediating international conflicts, negotiating cease-fires and treaties, and sending peacekeepers to war zones. As a country, it has shown a Metal's ability to create space for difficult conversations and seek alternatives to coercion and fighting, one of the most commendable traits in all of the Five

187

Elements. Switzerland is the oldest neutral country in the world; its neutrality was established by the Treaty of Paris in 1815 after the Napoleonic wars.

Just as Metal people foster change around them but resist getting in the middle of it, Switzerland itself has resisted progress: it was the last Western republic to grant women the right to vote. Some Swiss cantons (states) gave women the vote in 1959; it was granted at the federal level in 1971, and finally by the last cantons in 1990. And just as many Metal people are statuesque (or at least *look* tall), so is the nature of Switzerland. Forty-eight of Switzerland's mountains exceed 13,000 feet above sea level.

Metals Need to Have Systems

Metals promote structure and schedules while following doctrine and rules. Most public schools in the West are Metal organizations. They are steely and functional, and they focus on separating classes, grade levels, and the smart kids from the not-so-smart-kids. This model works for some people, but it also favors control and inflexibility over spontaneity and creativity.

The Western school system was created by Horace Mann and based on the German system. In 1806, after Prussia (the north German kingdom centered on Berlin) was defeated by Napoleon, its leaders decided that they had lost because soldiers had been thinking for themselves instead of following orders. Germans wanted to ensure that this would never happen again, so they created a strict eight-year system that taught duty, discipline, respect for authority, and obligation to follow orders. Kids were now told what to learn, what to think, and how long to think about it. By 1900, most countries in the Western world had adopted this system, which is very Metal (and Wood) and still reigns as the model for public schooling today.

Metals are often mechanical in the way they speak. There are very few peaks and valleys in their conversations, and it's hard to know if they've told a joke or not. They honor information over entertainment and appreciate protocol and excellence. The monotonous economics teacher in the 1980s film *Ferris Bueller's Day Off* is an example of this. He delivers an uninspired lecture in a dry and unengaging tone, oblivious to the fact that his students are falling asleep. Between points, he harangues students to respond by calling out, "Anyone, anyone?" He continues lecturing despite seeing students sound asleep and drooling on their desks. Here's a sample. Imagine this being delivered in a dry, clinical voice that never pauses for breath: "In 1930, the Republican-controlled House of Representatives, in an effort to alleviate the effects of the . . . anyone? anyone? . . . the Great Depression, passed the . . . anyone? anyone? . . . the tariff bill, the Hawley-Smoot Tariff Act, which . . . anyone?. . . raised or lowered? . . . raised tariffs, in an effort to collect more revenue for the federal government. . . ." If you were a teenager in the 1980s, you may remember the character very clearly (played by Ben Stein, who also had a lot of Water). If you weren't, you can check him out on YouTube, by Googling "Ferris Beuller economics teacher."

Metals Versus Woods: Two Practical Elements That Are Very Different

Metals and Woods are the most pragmatic, practical, and methodical elements, and so they are often associated with each other. However, they are very different

189

in all manners of style and demeanor. When something feels off for Metals in relationship, they can detach from people with little or no emotion. When something feels off for Woods, they need to express it (usually with anger), and if their communication effort isn't acknowledged, they can chop people out of their lives. Metals aren't known for their sense of humor; when they *are* funny, the wit is dry and sophisticated. Woods have a keen sense of humor that's laced with sarcasm. Metals tend to avoid conflict and tension with people. They don't want drama; it will just muddy their existence. Woods, on the other hand, enjoy a good debate and do not shy away from conflict or argumentation. With this in mind, it makes sense that many Metals are conscientious objectors, people who claim the right to refuse military service, beginning with Dutch Mennonites in 1575. Woods, on the other hand, are usually the first in line to volunteer for military service.

Metals and Woods are similar in that they are usually organized in work and feel comforted when they have control over situations. However, Metals don't feel the need to constantly be doing something, as Woods do—Metals can actually find a Zen space inside themselves, a move that's extremely difficult for Woods. Metals aren't hurried; in contrast, Woods are on a mission and are often pressing forward. Metals have a sense of composure and smoothly glide into a room like royalty. Woods are proud, bold, and not afraid to make a statement with a loud demeanor or strong opinions. When they enter a room, you know it.

When Metals get stressed, they get stuck in a loop of doing more and more of what is already not working, which is apparent to everyone but them. When Woods get stressed, they try to do everything themselves and, in bitterness and anger, get it done quickly and efficiently, without delegating help to anyone. This can be stressful for everyone around them. Metals are graceful and elegant, whereas Woods are strong and brazen. Metals want their projects done next; Woods want their projects done now. Metals are resolved; Woods are adamant. Metals are orderly; Woods are systematic. Metals are regulated; Woods are driven. Metals' energy is lithe; Woods' energy is solid. Metals' energy pulls in; Woods' energy is expansive. Metals are long-winded; Woods get to the point quickly and abruptly. Metals seem to live in the space between, as if they're in a sacred cathedral or walking a labyrinth. Woods dominate the space as if they own it. Metals act honorably because it's the right thing to do, even if people don't appreciate their efforts. Woods act honorably because it's the right thing to do, and they want credit for doing it.

If you have an emotionally healthy Metal and an emotionally healthy Wood, you have the kindest people in the Five Elements. They don't necessarily lead with niceness like Earths do through sweet salutations and heartfelt gratitude for everyone in their midst, but their kindness will become very apparent once you get to know them. They will be the first to give the shirt off their back, and they will have generosity like you have never known before.

Metals Are Full of Grace

The Metal way is a reverent way. The Metal person is a master at meeting life where it is and rising above it. Metals weather life's ups and downs without getting too ruffled. Not always, but many times they are spiritual seekers looking to the next guru or toward the next mind-body-spirit connection. If the most spiritually elevated gurus are in the high mountains of the Himalayas, that is where Metals will go. There is no argument, no controversy, and no debate: they will quietly go to where they find one-on-one connections with others who seem to also be on their path of higher consciousness.

Just as Metals aspire to higher causes, they want others to do so as well. They are interested in people reaching their personal best, and they will help you attain excellence if they are respectfully called upon.

Because Metals are often seeking a higher plane of spiritual existence or higher standards, if you don't fit into their vision of the divine, then they will probably politely end their relationship with you. Again, there is no arguing or struggle. Metals will say farewell and move on to something and someone at the level that they require. It can feel cold and detached, but for Metals, it is a path of the highest respect for themselves and their journey—and for you, as well. They can actually lose their self-respect if they continue to be a friend to a person who isn't resonating with their needs, desires, and path in life.

Jackie Kennedy—a Gracious Metal

Sometimes a celebrity shows characteristics of one element very strongly in public but a different element behind closed doors. Jacqueline Kennedy was the perfect Metal for the media. She had style, elegance, and grace. She once jokingly said, "Sex is bad because it rumples the clothes." (People close to Jackie said that she was very aware that her husband, John F. Kennedy, was a womanizer, but chose to ignore it and focus instead on assisting with his presidency.) Rising above the muck and choosing to ignore it is a very Metal quality.

The Kennedy family was very impressed by Jackie's calm, patience, composure, and intelligence. She never doubted or criticized her husband, even though she had her own thoughts and feelings about what he was up to. She helped to carefully craft her family's image and wouldn't do anything to disparage it. She was methodical and measured, answering hundreds of campaign letters for John, taping TV commercials, giving interviews, and writing a weekly newspaper column called "Campaign Wife," which was distributed nationally. Through all of this, she always maintained her dignity. She never boasted about her position in the world, even though she had been raised in a prominent New York family with wealth and status. She was the picture of graciousness, class, and sensibility.

Behind closed doors, however, Jackie most likely had a lot of Water and some Wood. She was passionate about reading (Water), was said by historian Ellen Fitzpatrick to have a "good deal of penetrating observation," and learned not to be ashamed of a real hunger for knowledge, which she often tried to hide (Water). She also had incredible dedication in everything she did, from raising her kids to helping with the presidency, as well as strong opinions (Wood) about her White House years. But she had Metal composure when reigning as First Lady, and most people would never know how many feelings, thoughts, and convictions were part of her personality, because she avoided speaking publicly about her personal life (Metal). She always exuded impenetrable sophistication.

With a Metal, Life Won't Revolve Around *You*

Sven was austere. Tall and lanky with angular features, he walked around the ashram as though floating an inch off the earth. In India, where I met him, his white robes always looked freshly laundered and ironed, like a well-tended saint's. His mind always seemed to be elsewhere. Back in Sweden, he spent endless hours crunching facts and figures for a computer company, and he was very good at it. But he felt called to India to embark on a spiritual journey to forge a closer connection with the divine. Sven was intellectual as well as spiritual. He was interested in divinity, bliss, and reaching higher levels of consciousness through yoga, meditation, and self-enlightenment.

Much to the dismay of others who had tried to relate to him, Sven seemed detached from emotions and feelings. He could come off as cold and even self-serving. That wasn't necessarily what Sven wanted, but it didn't really bother him either. Sven's existence wasn't about pleasing people, nor was it even about people. He respected others, and he found value in others, but there was a higher calling for Sven—something bigger than anything us mortals experience here on earth.

Metals want a cosmic connection with people—one-on-one, with complete mindfulness. They want to join together with people, but they aren't interested in chatty gossip or trite conversations. If they feel that a relationship with someone is shallow, then they will choose solitude instead. Receiving anything less than their ideal for a relationship, they may detach or simply not engage with that person any longer.

Being a Metal is a singular and very personal journey. In the Five Elements, they are the last element, so metaphorically they're in the final stage of a profound journey and don't have time to think of others. This can be difficult for people to understand, especially when one is close to a Metal who detaches and seems self-indulgent. However, on a broader level and in the bigger picture, Metals can be humanitarians. They want to make the world a better place by helping people, cities, and even countries. Though Metals aren't as prone as others to readily give of their heart and soul in one-on-one relationships, they are very altruistic, as evidenced by the frequency with which they give their money and time to charities. Volunteering for a few hours and then going back to their own life suits them. They are also charitable with money if they have the means, and can be very selfless. Angelina Jolie has promoted many causes, including women's rights, education, conservation, and aid for refugees. Mia Farrow is a UNICEF goodwill ambassador and helps organize extensive relief work in Darfur, Chad, and the Central African Republic. Princess Diana (who is also referred to in the Earth chapter, because she was very strong in both Metal and Earth) was heavily involved in the welfare of others, supporting dozens of charities, and often took the lead in the International Campaign to Ban Landmines. Audrey Hepburn devoted much of her life to UNICEF and worked in impoverished communities in Africa, South America, and Asia. Amal Alamuddin is a human-rights lawyer and activist who has worked on cases bringing to light the Armenian genocide, the Cambodian-Thai border dispute, and violations of the rules of war in the Gaza Strip during the Israel-Gaza conflict. All five of these women are powerful and beautiful, and all five have a strong presence of Metal element.

Metals tend toward perfectionism. In many aspects of their lives, they seem to be chipping away at rock to reveal precious gems. In business, they can distill the most complex details to get to the essential parts. In relationships, they repel the drama and illuminate the parts that really matter. As teachers and leaders, they can take input from many people and extract from it the essential information in its purest and most meaningful form. It's a unique and powerful skill. It simplifies life so that they can focus on those aspects that are most important for their personal evolution.

However, this quest for simple perfectionism can also be debilitating. Releasing the need to be perfect is an important lesson for Metals. Having learned it, they can live more joyfully and spontaneously. They will be more accepting of their faults, as well as those of others.

Being in Control Is Important for Metals

Metals feel good when they are held in high esteem. They do not assume the power in relationships with the intention of hurting anyone, but rather because of their high standards. Unfortunately, their standards of achievement can be unrealistic to everyone but them.

Madame Claudine was a top chef in a Michelin-starred restaurant called La Plaque Parfait (The Perfect Plate) in the South of France. She was focused on exact ingredients, specific measurements, and consistency of cooking. A "pinch" of salt would never do. Madame Claudine insisted on using silver measuring spoons leveled at the rim. Whereas other chefs throughout Europe were tossing their food into the air from a pan, Madame Claudine preferred to use more sophisticated techniques and proper utensils. She referred to sloppy techniques as "shoveling dirt." Each dish she presented was the finale of a choreography—carefully executed, clean, delicate, and elegant.

It was important to Madame Claudine that every customer could taste the simplicity of the food without being overwhelmed by extra sauces and side dishes. In fact, there were only three side dishes at her restaurant: apple-glazed carrots with fennel from the Pyrenees (four carrots, each two inches long), petite organic asparagus (three stalks, each four inches long), or a half ounce of summer sweet-pea flan. Her delicate entrées, like sea urchin with slivers of green chili and drops of yuzu on a crust of black bread, needed subtle accompaniments.

Madame Claudine's dining room and waitstaff were also immaculate. There were always fresh flowers, sparkling goblets, and spot-free windows. The well-mannered waiters and waitresses moved among the white-draped tables in sophisticated orchestration. They moved plates, glasses, forks, and knives carefully and attentively. They knew exactly when they were needed at a table. Of course, Madame Claudine had trained them all herself. She would glide through the restaurant with her head held high, saying nothing but always scanning for specks of dust, drooping flowers, or ruffled tablecloths. She never gave much praise to her staff about the hard work it took to make the restaurant a pristine environment for the rich and elegant to dine. Once she had eyed the dining room and notified the staff of corrections needed, she could be found in her kitchen—her kingdom, where she created perfect meals. The atmosphere in the kitchen was quiet, unruffled, and composed. She would have it no other way.

Healthy Metals know how to combine their quest for excellence with connections to people, even their employees and staff. My friend Inez runs a manufacturing facility and says that there is always the risk, as a Metal, to see her employees as automatons who are there to accomplish things for her and to be at her beck and call. It's not a conscious choice to treat people coldly or without respect; she's simply doing what she needs to do to run her business smoothly. Her team is not there to receive love. She assumes they have parents and friends for that.

When Metals notice that they're treating people with unbalanced superiority, they need to stop, take some deep breaths, and keep their standards in

197

check. Shifting from standards of perfection to standards that are workable for others will help all parties feel loved and respected. Taking deep, full inhales and exhales engages the lungs, expands the respiratory system, and softens the intestines to create more space and ease in the body (more on this in the next section). If Metals become unfriendly, formal, or stiff, engaging the lung energy can help release their need to command others. They can then quell their feelings of grief for not achieving their unachievable goal, voice their appreciation, and remember to show some gratitude for the people at hand.

Metals Become Displeased and Withdraw

Aurelia and Daphne were both performers in the world of dance, music, singing, and the arts. Daphne, a Wood, always wanted to know what made people tick. She wasn't afraid to ask people questions, and so she asked Aurelia, a Metal, where she was originally from. Aurelia responded quietly, in a wispy voice, that she never really landed in one city but went wherever she was guided.

Then Daphne asked what Aurelia did for her regular job. To Daphne this was a normal question to ask an artist. Performers always have another job—as waiters, bank tellers, gas station attendants, etc.—to pay the rent while they pursue their dreams. But Aurelia perceived the question as judgmental and shallow. Offended, she said, "Does it matter? How does what I do tell you about who I am? Our job titles don't define us as people."

Daphne was just trying to make small talk and felt shut down. But for Aurelia, labels and career titles were about the ego, and Daphne's innocent

198

question felt limiting and restrictive, not at all about who she was as a human being or her place here on earth.

Making small talk or asking polite but ultimately meaningless questions can irritate Metals. They don't enjoy talking about the small stuff. To them, life is much more spiritual than that. Once offended, Metals can ignore you and isolate themselves.

Metals Need to Stay Connected

When Metals are stressed-out, they will focus on some ideal scenario that they believe they could create if only they can analyze it exhaustively. A Metal who is a teacher may try to find a solution for student complacency by doing research and accumulating hundreds of facts on paper and in documents. She can forget that the most effective way to reach students is to talk to them, acknowledge them, and listen to them. Often getting nowhere with people by accumulating facts, Metals will then feel grief about their ineffectiveness. As one friend said, when her Metal husband gets stressed, he doggedly does more and more of what is already not working, whether it's trying to solve a problem in the workplace or trying to fix something that's broken at home. He gets caught in a loop. It's at those times that he also holds on to outworn belongings and ideas or habits that are difficult to shift.

The balancing factor for Metals who are devaluing others, themselves, and life experiences is companionship. Many times a Metal wants to be alone—the last thing they want to do is be around others when they're trying to find balance. They can go for days without speaking to anyone and without feeling

199

lonely (like a Water would). Self-reflection and going inward feels comforting, and so does work. But it is very important that they don't get lost in the constant evaluation and never-ending examination of their work or projects. I have a Metal friend who is an author and will plug away, working at his computer until he feels he has completed his self-imposed deadline. It doesn't matter if his wife has dinner on the table or the grandkids want him to play. He can't seem to pull himself away from the world of work inside his mind. He says he needs four to five hours a day on the computer with no interruptions and no breaks. His day usually starts about six A.M. The night before, he consciously focuses on the tasks for the next day and asks his deeper self to organize his approach to them. When he wakes up, before he gets out of bed, he thinks of the titles, the first sentence, and often the second sentence of the documents he needs to write. Then he walks directly to the computer—no breakfast, no shower, no shave. He doesn't check e-mail or answer the phone. His wife is not allowed to approach the office. Such efficiency is very admirable in business and in this Western world, where we give high approval ratings to disciplined people like Metals and Woods, but it can be very obsessive and rigid in the eyes of a partner.

Too much mental scrutiny can keep Metals in their heads and not in their hearts. People around them can start to give up on the idea that their relationships will ever be as important as the work that the Metals have planned. Relationships can wither and Metals must remember that it is communion with others that will bring them back to humanity, acceptance, and love.

A balanced and evolved Metal knows that long-term grief and detachment can be very unhealthy emotionally. They are fully aware that feeling emotions and being present during the highs and lows of relationships is not only appropriate, but also crucial for staying healthy and being able to keep their balance on the roller coaster of life.

DO!

- Do take time out every day to connect to a higher power.
- Do stay connected to people; Metals can become detached and ambivalent.
- Do find a way to experience joy and laughter, which will help keep your mind flexible.

DON'T!

- Don't walk away from people without acknowledging them and what they have said.
- Don't underestimate a person's feelings and how connected they feel to you.

Metals and Emotion: Grief

Metals' governing organs in traditional Chinese medicine are the lungs and the large intestine, and the emotion is grief. Another feeling that Metals often experience, or seek to experience, is spiritual enlightenment. One can attain spiritual enlightenment only if one is able to release and surrender. Letting go is one of the biggest lessons for Metals. Metal is the last element in the Five Element

201

wheel, and metaphorically it represents letting go so that one can die being OK with the fact that one hasn't finished all of one's projects or saved the world. It may help to think of autumn, the season of Metal. The leaves are falling, the sun is weaker, trees and animals are preparing to hibernate for winter, and people go through phases of letting go of the high energy and jubilance of the summer.

One of my best friends died when I was in my midtwenties. Her mom, who is very Metal, seemed to rise above her beloved daughter's tragic and unexpected death. At first it surprised me, and I wasn't sure what to think of it. As I drove up to her house a couple of days after the news, her mom slowly walked out to my car and met me at the gate. She was softly smiling and telling me that she knew how much her daughter meant to me, she knew how much I loved her, and she knew how hard this was for me. She put her arm around me and gently led me into the house. I was taken aback. I expected to be consoling her, holding her, and trying to find words of comfort for her. Instead, she found all the right words for me and was seemingly above the death. Over time I realized that a Metal often makes sense of a situation—even death—by chipping away at the obvious and finding the pure gems beneath. They find the value (that is imperceptible to the rest of us) even when the situations are traumatic. My best friend's mom noted what was valuable about her daughter and spoke of it eloquently and poetically while connecting to those things that her daughter loved—in this case, her daughter's relationships. The heavy emotions, endless crying, shock, and anger that often come with death aren't as apparent in Metals. Instead, they rise to the occasion with appreciation, embodiment, and grace. This is the magical, extraordinary gift that the Metals bring to our lives. They are often called

202

alchemists, and this is when the alchemist is most present, with their transformative, harmonizing, and healing work.

I have another friend who is a very evolved and wise Metal. She has spent her life working on herself to become a better person. She realized early on that there is never an end to the journey of self-improvement. She identified her blind spots, learned from people who inspired her, mastered relationship skills, and still focuses on positive outcomes for every day of her life. As a good Metal, she meditates. When someone close to her dies, her response is a masterful process to watch. She grieves graciously, speaking of all of the deceased's positive qualities and sharing their human challenges with humor and wit. She stays calm and takes much private time for herself. After she feels she is past the most difficult part of the grieving, she cleanses to create space in her life and renew. She goes on a complete physical, emotional, and mental cleanse. Physically, she stops eating all dairy, meat, and starches and ingests only broth and juice. She follows a schedule of yoga and stretching, as well as a lot of rest and colonics. It helps her emotionally to purge items from her home and car that are no longer necessary—old clothes, kitchen items, and even mementos that no longer serve her. She practices positive affirmations, prayer, and compassionate forgiveness. All of this cleansing is an exercise in letting go, grieving in a healthy way, and releasing the past so she can move on without the trauma becoming excess emotional baggage in her life.

Metals can attain moments of letting go through meditation, yoga, and spiritual quests. These moments can feel enlightened and perfect. Anything that is not perfect or enlightening can feel mundane and base to a Metal. Therefore, many yogis and gurus are Metals. They live a spiritual existence every day, a simple life of devotion, surrender, and nonattachment. Gurus get a bad rap in the West, where many self-proclaimed spiritual leaders have exploited their followers, but in other parts of the world, a guru is simply a revered guide or master who helps a person realize the potential of which the guru is already aware. A wonderful quality about Metals is that they are often inspirational sources who are willing to assess, guide, and help in the spiritual evolution of others, not just themselves.

Mahatma Gandhi—an Inspiring Metal

British rule in India lasted for more than one hundred years until India declared independence in 1947. In the early 1900s, Mahatma Gandhi, a lawyer by training, became a prominent leader in the Indian independence movement. He practiced nonviolent civil disobedience, a refusal to obey unjust, harmful laws by passively resisting their enforcement in order to bring wider attention to the injustice. It was a very Metal way of communicating dissatisfaction: no fighting, no violence.

Gandhi led campaigns across the country to build religious bridges between people, ease poverty, help oppressed ethnic groups, expand women's rights, achieve self-rule, and end untouchability. (There are more than 160 million people in India called Untouchables and deemed subhuman simply by virtue of where they were born in the Indian caste system, which for millennia has excluded this whole segment of people from society).

Gandhi inspired people to work for civil rights and freedom by going on hunger strikes to promote harmony, especially religious harmony. He was imprisoned many times in both South Africa and India but nevertheless practiced nonviolence in every experience and always advocated that others do the same.

As many Metals do, Gandhi carefully chose the people whom he wanted in his life. He was also very mindful about his thoughts. He said, "I will not let anyone walk through my mind with their dirty feet." Likewise, Gandhi lived as many Metals live—modestly and self-sufficiently. He ate simply, was a vegetarian, and undertook self-purification rituals like fasting. He dressed simply, spoke simply, and lived spiritually. These are the traits of a strong Metal, and Gandhi was one of the finest representations of this element.

Metals and the Body

Metals are usually tall and svelte, or at least they look tall. They often appear to be stiff or inhibited (men more commonly than women), as if they aren't comfortable in their own skin. They receive contact awkwardly and are sometimes indifferent to physical sensation. Metals tend to have high cheekbones and sculpted facial features. Their walk is slow and smooth, as if they're floating an inch or two off the earth.

Metals dress simply, in comfortable fabric and materials that suit their high standards. They prefer muted colors to bright or dark ones. They often wear white, in soft materials like silk, brushed linen, and light-weight fleece, because, as in their emotional world, they don't want to deal with anything too heavy.

The large intestine (colon) and the lungs are the dominant organs for Metals. The large intestine is about five feet long and removes substances from

205

the body that it no longer needs. Its energy is directly connected to the lungs. Most people do not breathe deeply enough to fully expand the lungs and maintain vibrant respiratory and eliminatory systems. It's no coincidence that shallow breathers often have constipation.

Breathing all the way down into the belly helps the internal organs, including the large intestine, to function well. Herbs, healthy eating, and colon irrigation can also help. A clogged colon can be the source of health problems as various as asthma, acne, arthritis, migraines, and weight gain. Keeping it clean and healthy prevents illness.

Breathing deeply also helps the respiratory, lymphatic, immune, circulatory, digestive, and nervous systems to work better. In addition, breathing deeply relaxes the body, helps with concentration, releases endorphins (internal painkillers), promotes good sleep, and increases the strength and flexibility of the joints. Moreover, improved circulation helps keep wrinkles at bay and create beautiful skin!

Samuel Couldn't Breathe or Poop

Samuel had experienced lots of loss during his forty-eight years of life. He lost both parents in a car accident when he was a teenager, and several of his friends had passed away. He was estranged from his sister, and he drifted further away from any social life as the years went on. He wasn't processing his grief well; he dealt with it by isolating himself. He ate the same things every day. He had a couple of pieces of toast, some coffee, and usually pasta for din-

206

ner. He ate very few fruits, vegetables, or protein-rich foods, and he drank very little water. He became focused on his work and his meditation. He awoke at 5:00 A.M. every day to meditate for two hours, worked for most of the day as a manager at the local morgue, and meditated again before bed.

Samuel seemed in good physical health. He was trim and tall. But on a closer look, his skin was ashen and his hair was a dull gray. He looked old for his forties. He always seemed to have a slight cough, which was getting worse over time and becoming chronic. He found himself having to catch his breath. Samuel also had a large tummy despite being tall and lanky. He also had constipation, which he thought was a part of getting older, so he just learned to live with it. There were days when he would have coughing fits for most of the morning while holding his tight stomach and wishing he could have a bowel movement.

Samuel had no semblance of a social circle except for his Fire sister, Bobbi, who would visit sometimes, despite his ill will toward her. On one occasion, Bobbi insisted on staying. She replaced his meals of white toast and refined pasta with organic, fresh, and free-range foods. She encouraged him to drink lots of water throughout the day and to add deep breathing to his meditation practice. She even convinced Samuel to do a colonic. Before long, Samuel's cough was gone, and he was having regular bowel movements. His hair was shinier, his face had more color, and his mood had lifted. He actually looked forward to his days. Instead of just meditating, he started deep-breathing exercises and regular walking in nature. He also combined positive affirmations with his meditations. He soon met a woman who was very accepting and compassionate, an Earth/Fire, a sweet combination to help Samuel bring his spirit back.

207

YOUR LARGE INTESTINE LOVES THESE FOODS

- Juicy fruits and vegetables
- Honey
- Walnuts
- Spinach

YOUR LUNGS AND LARGE INTESTINE LOVE THESE HERBS

- Aloe vera (both)
- Garlic (both)
- Senna leaf (large intestine)
- Black cohosh (large intestine)

Movement for Metals

Metals usually do very well at slow, smooth movement, as in Tai Chi and yoga. However, as with all the elements, Metals need not only to do what feels natural, but also to stretch outside their comfort zone. Metals need to raise their heart rates for better circulation. More balanced exercise will also promote deeper breathing.

Most Metals will not feel comfortable with exercise as part of a team. Nor will a Metal feel comfortable with competitive sports, preferring solitary endeavors in which the exercise becomes a type of meditation. That is why yoga feels so right to Metals.

Eden Energy Medicine Exercise for Metals:
Connecting Heaven and Earth

Breathing and stretching with one hand up toward the sky and the other down toward the ground can be soothing and calming for Metals; plus, it's a powerful stretch for the hips, waist, and torso. It is very refreshing and can help bring you back into inspiration when you are living too much in your head. This is one of the most popular exercises in Eden Energy Medicine because it makes people feel so good.

1. Inhale through your nose, bring your arms out and then together into prayer position. Exhale through your mouth.
2. Inhale through your nose again, and stretch one arm up and one arm down, pushing with your palms.
3. Hold, exhale through your mouth, and return to the prayer position. Switch arms and repeat four or five times.

Finding Balance as a Metal

Metals are often drawn to places like India to develop their spiritual lives or to "find themselves." Not all Metals are spiritual but many are, with an emphasis on nirvana, bliss, the afterlife, and experiences of oneness. They often go on spiritual retreats or pilgrimages, as they want to learn to transcend the ego, move beyond fear of change, tune in to intuition, and surrender to life's uncertainties. Spiritual work can put them in touch with God, Goddess, spirits, and guides that can help them through the rest of their days here on earth, changing their lives in the most profound ways.

In late December 2006, I traveled to India to perform at a large resort and usher in the new year. The White Sands Resort in Goa was immaculate and beautiful. A small wooden house had been built for me on the beach; I had my own private guard at my beck and call and meals and sweets whenever I wanted. I was also treated to day trips on elephants, visits to crystal rivers, Ayurvedic massages with elixirs specially made for my skin, hair, and eyes. I was treated like a queen (a Metal would have loved it). Outside the resort, however, was the worst poverty I had ever seen. I witnessed men with no limbs rolling down the streets on makeshift dollies. I saw small children perched on top of garbage heaps eating whatever they could find, even though everything was covered in maggots. I was confronted by hundreds of beggars with no teeth, some with no eyes, skin wounds that I had seen only in horror films, and bones protruding through their thin, dark skin. I saw a dead body in a ditch on a main street; people simply ignored it.

The extreme contrast between this heart-wrenching misery and my pampered life as a celebrity performer confounded me. I couldn't make sense of it.

210

Every day I found myself in tears, wondering what on earth India was about and why people revered it so much. My Water was drowning in confusion and my Wood was raging with anger.

One morning, while drinking a lassi (a yogurt and fruit smoothie) and watching peacocks parade on the resort grounds, I struck up a conversation with a man at a nearby breakfast table. I asked Arthur, a Metal, where he was from, what he was doing in India, and how long he would stay. He said he had come to India to simply *be*, and he would stay until he was drawn to leave. He spoke about transcendence in a breathy voice and said India was the most important place on earth. He told me he had been fasting on water for days and planned to only eat raw fruits and vegetables. He owned one small bag of belongings—two white flowing shirts, two pairs of linen pants, a small fold-up yoga mat, and some toiletries. He didn't need to bring a sweater, even for the cold mountain regions of India, because he had learned to cool and heat his body through mindful thought.

Arthur continued to praise India as the most spiritually evolved place on earth until my Wood kicked in. What about India's archaic caste system, which considers some people so low class that they can work only with sewage, dung, and dead animals? What about the oppressive poverty? Child hunger in India is deemed worse than in Africa. What about India's failure to prosper, even though it has been free of colonial rule for almost seventy years? What about the rapes and gang rapes of women in the lower- and middle-class castes and of female tourists? What about the grotesque male chauvinism?

Arthur told me I needed to rise above all that—the poverty, the oppression, and the caste system. "Everyone has a place on earth," he said, referencing Hinduism, Buddhism, and his own religious dogma. Who was I to meddle in

211

that divine plan? He told me that I needed to purify my thoughts. "If your mind is dirty, how can your soul shine?" he said, quoting the Indian guru Yogaswami. He even went as far as telling me that I was an unevolved person because I allowed things to bother me. India was the right place for me, he said, to deal with my ego, my anger, and my inability to let go.

Arthur was a Metal out of balance. His desire to rise above this earthly plane was so focused that he had lost his ability to connect to people—the poor people all around him or even a fellow traveler at his hotel making conversation. I felt it was unlikely that Arthur would ever reach the spiritual perfection he sought. For Metals, working on their own growth as people will more likely lead them to discover what they need to be fulfilled.

Metals need to remember that being human and being here on earth is an imperfect dance, and it always will be. Imperfection is part of the beauty of being human, and accepting that fact can be part of the transition out of an ego-driven state. To become one with the divine isn't about being indifferent to people; it's accepting that we are all imperfect, we all struggle, and some of us (including Metals) need assistance. And that's OK.

Metals are at their best when they can open up to the wonders of people, with all of their faults, just as they open up to the wonders of something beyond the human realm. Truly appreciating and acknowledging another person by spending time together, having conversations, and offering companionship makes a connection far beyond what we can see, a connection of the heart. Good intentions and love, not to mention new neuronal pathways, are created when people truly connect.

A Metal in balance is inspiring! Everyone wants to experience the heavenly existence to which Metals seem to connect. Aligned, Metals give off a sublime "perfume" of the divine. They live in great consciousness and can make people everywhere feel honored, uplifted, respected, and healed.

Barack Obama is an example of a man who makes people feel honored, uplifted, respected, and healed. He has many qualities of the Metal element, from the sense of stillness and dignity, to his eyes that seem to be searching for something beyond the commonplace. Also revealed in his eyes is an underlying grief, which is so common in Metals. There is grief for what hasn't been accomplished, grief for a life that ticks away out of all control, and grief for things that come to an end—that is, all things. It's interesting that one of the complaints about him is that he doesn't socialize with Congress. This is typical of Metal, which is not a social element and doesn't feel bound to obligatory duties.

EXERCISE TO BALANCE METALS
- Dancing of any kind (Metals need to get out of their heads and into their bodies)
- Movement with friends
- Stretching

CALM YOUR METAL
- Stop and breathe
- Take four or five slow, deep breaths
- Shut your eyes
- Rest your mind

BALANCE YOUR LUNGS AND LARGE INTESTINE

- Acupuncture
- Acupressure
- Eden Energy Medicine

Metals in Relationship

Laura loved Michael, but trying to get a firm commitment from him was frustrating. One day he finally agreed to move in together. He wasn't ready for marriage, but they could cohabitate, he said. Laura and Michael had dated for over a year, so Laura knew he was tidy and didn't have many possessions. She was also drawn to his spiritual nature and liked the part of him that wasn't attached to the material world.

However, as Laura started moving her boxes into Michael's home, he became increasingly uncomfortable. He didn't want her stuff around—or any stuff around. Laura suddenly noticed that Michael had almost no furniture, and what he did have was wood or metal that didn't invite touch or promise comfort. In fact, it all had an almost repellent effect. There was a dining table with hard chairs and a sitting area with two hard meditation pillows. To round out the large, spacious house, there was a futon, a computer, three books, a tablet, and a pen. When she went into the bathroom to fill the cabinets, she found a natural bristle toothbrush and a small container with what looked like homemade toothpaste. Where was the soap and all the other bathroom things?

She couldn't figure it out. Every cabinet she opened was almost empty. She migrated to the kitchen with her boxes of plates, mugs, and refrigerator magnets. The kitchen had a juicer and a couple of glasses, five forks, and two plates. Food was sparse in the refrigerator. There was some green stuff that looked like kale and some almond milk. A Tibetan prayer flag hung across the kitchen window, one of the only decorations in the whole house.

Laura asked Michael if he had a storage unit. He did not. Where were all his photo albums, music, knickknacks, and letters collected from fifty years of living? He didn't have any. Michael talked to Laura softly about possessions and the weight of them on a person's soul. He reminded her that he always had memories of the past but that holding on to the past was unhealthy for the mind and body. It could only get in the way of being in the *now*. Yearbooks, mementos from trips, letters from past relationships, sentimental jewelry, decorative paintings, and polished china only pulled him back to the past. Not to mention that it cluttered the house, and when the house is cluttered, the mind is cluttered, not free. According to Michael and many other Metals, too much stuff is overstimulating. It provokes feelings of anxiety. The Metal home is a sparse and spacious home. The comfy overstuffed pillows and knickknacks are for the Earth types.

A relationship with a Metal can be challenging, but remember, most people aren't pure Metals; most people are a combination of two or three elements, which temper one another so they won't be so extreme, even if one element is very strong. However, if you do want romance with fireworks, excitement, and a place for all your stuff, a Metal may not be the one for you. The relationship will be more sublime and mild than enthralling and passionate. A Metal finds love and connection in subtlety and the big picture, rather than in delightful little details that other folks may wait for or expect.

When Metals are at their best, they are interested in helping people reach their personal best, and they can have a soothing effect on people. Because they don't want to get entangled in issues and problems, they remain focused on the peaceful outcome and anything worthwhile that can be gleaned from the situation. As Metals, they are interested in finding the gold in the relationship, the quality that will keep it together and growing in a positive direction. That gold—the magic that keeps the two of you connected—can feel like a cosmic connection, something greater and bigger than what our eyes can see. Metals help guide situations and people by inspiration and wisdom—not fear—and they make the world a better place.

It is important for Metals to always remember to do routine maintenance on their connections with their partners. A Metal needs to check in often to find out what her partner needs and desires, hear what he or she says, and work to establish mutual give-and-take. Otherwise, it's too easy for Metals to retreat to a solitary world inside their minds. If they allow themselves to become too detached, they may no longer notice what their mate needs or is experiencing.

Every element benefits from reminders to connect to others, but Metals need to be extra conscious to pull themselves out of rigidity and honor the people around them. Metals can post reminders for themselves in the form of yellow sticky notes on their computers with brief messages like, "Stop what you are doing and tell your mate that you love her/him." Another could be, "Take a break. Take five deep breaths. Now get up and kiss your mate on the cheek. You don't need a reason." These simple reminders may seem stupid or shallow to a Metal, but to her or his partner, they show care, understanding, and a deep desire to connect. They can make a difference.

216

If you're in a relationship with a Metal, it helps to *schedule* meals and fun, reminding them that this time to connect is important to you. Metals may consider a handful of nuts or a few carrots here and there a complete meal. They will want to come to a completion point with their projects before they take a break, so stopping for dinner will not be a priority. But you can make a connection to them easier by setting specific times to eat together and take breaks. When Metals are late, go easy on them, but don't placate them. While they will try to keep working and not necessarily make you a priority, they also need to know that being late is disrespectful. Be firm with boundaries.

If you're wondering how to make Metals happy, you may need to reframe the question. Ask instead how to help them feel free or even blissful. Their answer may surprise you—it may be as simple as taking a walk in a beautiful setting or doing a mindful meditation together. Joy and happiness for a Metal looks very different from joy and happiness for the other elements. Don't expect Metals to skip around, jump up and down, or shout out in glee when they are happy. They may just give a soft smile and a gentle nod of the head.

Metals need to be one with a higher vibration here on earth. They need to connect to the present moment. They also do very well in service to a person or a group of people. Church, temple, or spiritual groups and houses of worship are where Metals feel at home. It is always wise to encourage them to join a small group of people working to make this planet a better place. They will vibrate at a higher frequency if you do.

217

Do You Know a Metal?

Do you have a Metal in your life? Are you in a relationship with a Metal? When someone remains undisturbed and disengaged, with the ability to speak eloquently under extreme circumstances, you will know you have a Metal on your hands.

Metals enjoy solitude, serenity, and reverence. They want to connect with people but aren't drawn to big crowds or social circles. They want to connect one-on-one with you, and then they want their freedom to be alone, work, or connect with the divine.

If you want a wise friend who has a keen perspective on life and loss, as well as virtue and detachment, befriend a Metal. A Metal in your life will ask for your company and be deeply grateful when you give it. The bonus is that when you give of your time and company to a Metal, you don't just receive friendship, but they also help you become a better human being. Such a person will feel that you are a precious gem and will help you become aware of your unique value to this world.

You May Be a Metal If . . .

You may be a Metal if you feel that you are on a singular path in life with very few people who understand you. Do you feel pulled toward spirituality and something beyond your own existence? Do you feel resolved about your choices and unwilling to accept that others know what is right for you? Do you work slowly and methodically until your tasks are completed? Are you a good friend when the relationship is one-on-one and steered to what you feel is important? If you are sitting quietly and meditating on these ideas, thinking that this may be true of you, you may be a Metal.

IF YOU THINK YOU ARE A METAL . . .

○ Remember that for many people, joy is real. Don't analyze it just because you don't feel the same heightened emotions.

○ You probably engage in some sort of spiritual practice, such as meditation, prayer, or mindfulness. The fact that others don't doesn't mean they're unevolved.

○ Expressing anger isn't necessarily bad. Expressing anger can be healthy, especially if the person expressing it feels acknowledged and the person receiving it gains understanding.

○ Avoid being so in your head and in your own thoughts that you can no longer connect with others.

○ Don't be blinded by your quest for peace and bliss. When your searching becomes so focused on you and your own journey, you will miss out on people and experiences around you.

○ Discard the assumptions. Someone may not look the part of a person you would consider sophisticated, evolved, or intelligent, but that doesn't mean they aren't.

○ Remember, when you don't share your emotions with people, you appear snotty and holier-than-thou. Sharing your real emotions feels good—and it humanizes you.

○ Crying is OK. Feeling grief is OK.

○ Observe yourself from the inside and the outside. Are you being aloof and indifferent? If so, people will get the message to stay away from you and not engage.

○ When people talk to you, they appreciate a response. If you just listen and then walk away, the experience can be surreal for others. They may feel that they have wasted your time (or theirs). Even if they did waste your time, it's important to acknowledge that they communicated with you.

○ Do something that makes you laugh hard or cry hard. Feel deeply. You may be uncomfortable at first, but doing so will open your heart and get you out of your head. It's good for you.

Metal Personality Assessment Quiz

Take the following quiz to find out how strong you are in the Metal element. Chances are that you're a combination of elements. This means some of these answers will be true for you, and some won't. Understanding, accepting and working with the elements that compose your personality are crucial steps in understanding the actions and motivations of others and being at peace with yourself.

Rate the following statements according to your tendencies. On a scale of 1 to 5, 1 is never true and 5 is always true. When you are finished, add up your scores and compare them with your scores for the other elements. A high score may mean that you have found your primary element. You are led by your primary element (or shared primary elements), which will dominantly reveal those respective traits in your personality, but you will be very influenced by your secondary, and to a lesser degree, third, fourth, and fifth elements. In certain circumstances you may draw on elements as a coping mechanism or strategy, but they may not be heavily present in your day-to-day life like your primary element(s).

1	2	3	4	5
Never True	Almost Never True	Sometimes	Almost Always True	Always True

Are You a Metal?

UNDER STRESS I EXPERIENCE THE FOLLOWING:

_____ Sudden sleepiness

_____ Inability to have fun

_____ A need to be the master

_____ Respiratory difficulties

_____ Constipation

_____ A critical attitude

_____ Emotional iciness

_____ Aloofness

_____ Rigidity

IN GENERAL:

_____ My personal lifestyle is orderly and simple.

_____ I control my environment.

_____ I find what is off-kilter and strive to slowly transform it.

_____ I hold myself and others to the highest standards.

_____ I like everyone I work with to follow proper protocol.

_____ I like systematic tasks that require logic.

_____ I think of myself as an exemplary human being.

_____ I avoid conflict.

_____ I can be very long-winded and I don't get to the point quickly.

_____ I am very comfortable not doing anything and just being mindful of the space I am in.

_____ I analyze joy and question enthusiasm.

_____ Integrity and excellence are extremely important to me.

_____ I am self-contained and intellectually independent.

_____ I am not an overseer of other people's lives and I don't meddle in their affairs.

_____ When someone has more competence than I do, I can accept their expertise.

_____ Ethics and reason have more pull for me than pleasure and fun.

_____ I wait my turn, I take my time, and then I state my opinions precisely with little emotion.

222

_____ I get rid of what I don't need and my emotions are not tied to my personal possessions.

_____ I am correct and fair.

_____ I hold myself back when it comes to expressing my feelings.

_____ When I speak, I speak softly.

_____ I often sit still and straight with excellent posture.

_____ When I walk, dance, or move I seem to calmly glide.

_____ For exercise I am drawn to fluid movement like yoga, Tai Chi, and ballet.

_____ Sometimes I forget to eat.

_____ I am not easily swayed or influenced to change course, even by failure.

_____ I don't have a lot of keepsakes like love letters or items that evoke nostalgia.

_____ I am aware of time but finishing my tasks is more important than being timely.

_____ I hunger for what seems to be an unattainable spiritual connection.

_____ I sometimes feel incapable of letting myself go.

_____ I often feel grief over life.

_____ People have accused me of being holier-than-thou.

_____ I crave distance and solitude, yet I want meaningful relationships.

223

_____ I do well in jobs where I can work alone or one-on-one; I don't do well in customer service.

_____ I believe that less is more.

_____ I don't understand the importance of trinkets and mementos.

_____ I have a hard time believing that unabashed happiness is real.

_____ I am uncomfortable with clutter and "shelf pollution."

_____ I follow rules and protocols and feel no reason to break them.

_____ I believe that to connect with people, words are not always needed.

_____ I do what is honorable, and I don't need to be acknowledged in return.

_____ I can be very patient. I am not comfortable with rushing.

TYPICAL PROBLEMS FOR A METAL:

_____ I isolate myself from people to get to my work.

_____ I rank people by how much quality they have.

_____ I can be arrogant.

_____ I can be indifferent and dismissing.

_____ I can be inappropriately formal and stiff.

_____ I can be nitpicky.

_____ I continue to work doggedly at something even when it isn't successful for me or anyone else.

_____ I analyze things to death.

224

_____ I can be dogmatic and calmly stubborn.

_____ I am often described as aloof and distant.

_____ I cannot switch easily from intellectual projects to human encounters.

_____ I can get stuck in the details in my head, preventing me from seeing the big picture.

_____ I am inhibited and don't feel free in my body.

_____ I can be insensitive.

_____ **SCORE FOR METAL**

CHAPTER 6

Now That You Know Your Element—a Deeper Look
Keys to Understanding the Yin-Yang of Relationships

■

W HILE WE ALL HAVE a dominant element, we are also influenced by our second and third elements. Knowing how these elements operate in combination with other elements (in ourselves and others) brings insight to all aspects of our lives—our relationships, our work, and our worldview.

When discussing the Five Elements—which I do with my family on a daily basis—we say people *lead* with an element. In other words, people express one element in most interactions throughout the day, at work or home, in public or private, but they may have another strong element, which comes out at home with their family. Either one could be their primary element, or the two could be equal.

When we recognize the slow pace of Water, the anger of Wood, the explosive energy of Fire, the codependency of Earth, or the detachment of Metal, we begin to understand that the energy of the elements ebbs and flows through each of us. These energies are not meant to pigeonhole us, but rather to allow us to generate compassion for ourselves and for others. Under stress we might

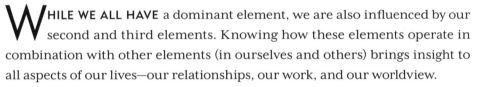

slip into a secondary or even tertiary element, and it can come on very strong. Or we might present one element in public but another one behind closed doors.

None of the elements in our makeup—primary, secondary, or tertiary—is less genuine or less "us." Having more than one strong element makes us diverse and well rounded. When we understand this, our differences then begin to seem normal instead of annoying, irritating, or wrong (though Woods will still be irritated). We can celebrate each other's strengths and be OK with our differences. Likewise, we have more freedom to be ourselves because we are more aware that differences are necessary. No one should ever be forced to be someone she or he is not.

You may even have fourth and fifth elements that are hibernating until you access them. They pop out only occasionally. For instance, I am a Wood/Water/Earth. Wood is my strongest element, but I have a Water/Earth body and often lead with Water in public, which is apparent when I get shy. My Wood often comes out under stress and in my work. I can confidently say that Fire is my fourth element and that I have almost never felt Metal in my life. However, people who have seen me joking, smiling, and laughing onstage or in the limelight may think my primary element is Fire, because that's when some of my Fire comes out. I also get lit up by being around other Fires, like my mom or my sister. If I'm not too much in my Wood or Water, they can sweep me into a wonderland of glittery sparks of joy and authentic bouts of laughter.

You will find an interesting combination of the elements within yourself, just as I have. You may be strong in one element all day, until you get into the comfort of your home and can be your "real self." You might be strong in one element but have the body type of your secondary or tertiary element (you may be a short Metal). You also may have a yin or yang nature in your element. Knowing if a person is yin or yang can be a real game changer; it can mean the difference, for instance, between a Wood being aggressively up in someone's face or just mildly assertive (see Yin and Yang, page 238).

Will We Be a Match Made in Heaven or a Disaster Waiting to Happen?

There are many reasons why relationships do or don't work between two people—more than just the influence of the Five Elements. A major reason is how a person was raised by their parents or caretakers. For instance, a person may naturally be a Wood element. But if their innate Wood traits get squashed when they are young by a family member who expects a child to obey authority and not speak unless they are spoken to, then their Wood traits may not be apparent until they are older. Unfortunately, by the time they are an adult, if they have been intensely controlled all their lives, their Wood personality may not present in a healthy way. Likewise, Fire children are often told to "settle down," "be still," or—even worse—diagnosed with ADD when they may simply have a very energetic disposition from being a Fire element. It can be confusing for a Fire child to be tamed by adults, and this confusion may play out when they are older and in their own adult relationships.

Other reasons why a person does well or not so well in a relationship may be their astrological makeup, the pulse of society at the time of the relationship, their ethnic culture, the stress levels of the two individuals, outside influences of other friends and family, the partners' experiences, values, beliefs,

229

and spirituality, and finally their sensory types—whether they perceive the world as a tonal, visual, kinesthetic, or digital type. There is no way to predict how your element will or won't get along with another element, but we can make some generalizations about how the Five Elements combine with each other in relationships.

Elements That Flow Together

The following elements are on each other's "flow cycles." They will combine well with each other, and their relationships will probably be fairly smooth. Of course, there are no guarantees, but if you are in one of the combinations below, you might notice that, no matter what, you just like each other and there is an ease to your partnership even when you aren't getting along perfectly.

WATER SUPPORTS WOOD

Waters and Woods can be incredibly productive together. They can make a great team, especially in business. The Water comes up with inspirational ideas, and the Wood puts them into action. However, a Wood can become very frustrated with a Water's slow rhythm, and in the presence of the big, fast Wood energy, a Water may retreat.

Opportunity: The Water can help the Wood to slow down and go with the flow. The Wood can help the Water to be productive and meet deadlines.

WOOD SUPPORTS FIRE

Woods and Fires have great chemistry. The Wood will appreciate the Fire's magical ability to spread celebratory joy, and the Fire will appreciate the Wood's knack for staying on task. However, the Wood may not be up for the high drama and capricious nature of the Fire, and the Fire may not like the strong doses of reality, detailed orders, and time signals that the Wood is bound to give.

Opportunity: The Wood can help the Fire to focus and stay on track. The Fire can help the Wood to relax and have fun.

FIRE SUPPORTS EARTH

Fires and Earths are natural supporters of each other's joy. This relationship will be very warm and loving. The Earth will feel motivated and thrilled by the Fire energy, and the Fire will feel grounded by the Earth. Difficulties come if the Earth gets overwhelmed by the Fire's high energy or if the Fire feels suffocated by the Earth's tendency to parent a partner and slip into codependency.

Opportunity: The Fire can help the Earth to let go of the past and be in the present. The Earth can help the Fire by providing support and calm so the Fire doesn't burn out.

EARTH SUPPORTS METAL

This even-keeled relationship can be very beautiful. Metals are nurtured by Earths, and Earths feel protected by Metals. The Metal will appreciate the

231

Earth's natural compassion and ability to flow with social events, and the Earth will drink up the Metal's wisdom and role as a mentor, especially when the Metal helps the Earth to get unstuck and out of her comfort zone to create change. However, if the Metal starts to feel suffocated by the Earth, the Metal may detach. If the Earth feels too controlled by the Metal, the Earth may become anxious.

Opportunity: The Earth can help the Metal to stay connected to people, even when the Metal is under stress and tempted to detach emotionally. The Metal can help the Earth by understanding that some detachment is OK, that it can provide solitude and emotional clarity.

METAL SUPPORTS WATER

There is a peacefulness between Metals and Waters. It's not a bouncy, happy relationship like that of two college girlfriends, but more like a deep friendship between two old men who enjoy sitting on a bench swapping sage ideas. It is a meeting of the minds, as the Water searches for meaning and the Metal seeks enlightenment. Water is a new beginning (the first in the Five Elements wheel), and Metal is the ending (the last in the wheel), so they are good at both beginning new projects and completing them, instead of letting them fizzle out before fruition. However, most Metals are neat-freaks and Waters don't mind messes and all the *stuff*. The relationship could fall apart when these opposing preferences aren't resolved in a comfortable compromise.

Opportunity: The Metal can help the Water detach from *things* and finish projects. The Water can help the Metal connect to people and not detach.

232

The Button Pushers

When two elements are on each other's "control cycle," things can become difficult. Just as energy has polarity, a push and a pull (think of magnets), so do the elements. The control cycle can feel like two elements pushing against each other, and pushing each other's buttons, even when they also have a lot of respect for each other—at least superficially. There may be no obvious reasons to feel irritated, frustrated, exasperated, hurt, or angry, but those feelings may very well come bubbling up around someone whose element pushes all of your element's buttons. You might feel that all of your vulnerabilities and deepest control issues surface too.

WATER CONTROLS FIRE

A Water and a Fire are almost exact opposites. At first a Fire will feel supported by a Water because of the great ideas and robust beginnings that a Water brings to projects. A Water will revel in the excitement, warmth, and love that a Fire brings. However, the Fire can easily start to feel that the Water is a wet blanket suppressing fun and may seek more social interaction with others. This could bring up a Water's tendency toward low self-esteem and abandonment issues. A Water may feel abandoned by Fire's gregarious tendencies and hopeless about preserving the relationship.

Promote Harmony: Water can promote harmony by allowing for Fire's energetic nature, which will help Fire to feel the sense of freedom that she loves. Fire can take time to slow down and enjoy some mellow activities with Water, which will make the Water feel seen and acknowledged.

233

FIRE CONTROLS METAL

Fires and Metals have very different natures and ways of seeing the world. A Fire is heart centered and emotional, whereas a Metal doesn't always show emotion in words, expressions, or gestures. If these two elements can accept their expressive differences, they might enjoy an incredible connection full of playfulness and fun, as well as reverence and solitude.

Promote Harmony: A Fire can promote harmony by slowing down and listening in the presence of a Metal, while resisting the tendency to interrupt during conversation. The Metal can promote harmony by allowing the Fire to be spirited and energetic without analyzing the enthusiasm.

METAL CONTROLS WOOD

Logically, this relationship seems a good match. Metals and Woods are structured, powerful people. However, both tend to be bright, feel that they alone are correct, and indulge in power plays. In addition, a Metal may make a Wood feel small and controlled. Ultimately, it will be difficult for the Wood to not feel angry and the Metal to not detach.

Promote Harmony: The Metal can promote harmony by acknowledging the Wood, recognizing her strengths, and stating those strengths through affirming words. The Wood can promote harmony by making the Metal feel seen, with encouraging words of meaningful connection and friendship.

WOOD CONTROLS EARTH

When first getting to know each other, Woods can find Earths' compassion endearing, and Earths can find Woods' structure motivating. A Wood does well under pressure, and an Earth may respect that fortitude, but the pressure can also be threatening to an Earth, who generally doesn't like fast changes. An Earth can end up resenting the competitive nature of a Wood, and a Wood might try to force an Earth to have more drive.

Promote Harmony: A Wood can promote harmony by being gentle with an Earth and not speaking loudly or sharply, especially about timelines, plans, and schedules. An Earth can promote harmony by communicating wants and needs clearly, so there is no ambiguity for the Wood.

EARTH CONTROLS WATER

Initially an Earth and a Water can do well together. They like the idea that they can be themselves because they feel comfortable, safe, and nurtured. Unfortunately, their relationship can also feel muddy. An Earth can cater to a Water's indecisiveness, causing imbalance that can inspire doubt in a Water who already struggles with fear and trust. A Water's doubt can block her ability and desire to be intuitive, and this can lead to bitterness.

Promote Harmony: An Earth can promote harmony by not appeasing a Water, by not forgetting her own needs and desires. A Water can promote harmony by giving the Earth the time she needs to avoid hasty decisions and listen to her own wee voice.

235

Double Trouble or Twice Blessed?

It's uncommon to find two of the same elements in a lasting relationship, perhaps because it really is true that opposites attract each other at first. When a one-element relationship does happen, it can feel like watching identical twins interact.

WATER AND WATER

Two Waters can form a relationship that will probably be deep and philosophical, exchanging great ideas that fill the atmosphere like a meteor shower. Like meteor showers, those ideas will disappear before they get to earth. These ideas floating about in the ether and not being put into action will cause the Waters to become melancholy and hopeless. All relationships need some uplifting, productive moments, and this may be one in which very little gets done and the plot lacks energy and vigor.

The Friend in Need or the Therapist to Choose: A Metal. A Metal will be able to resonate with the slow flow of the Waters' and can be detached enough to pull the two out of their depth and get them on the right path to meet their goals.

WOOD AND WOOD

Most Woods love themselves, love being Woods, and love other Woods. They will get along great and be extremely productive, efficient, and respectful of each other. Timelines will be met, and worlds will be conquered. But having two generals and no subordinates isn't a lot of fun. It's all work and conquer, work and conquer. Two Woods together will lack play, creativity, and vacations.

The Friend in Need or the Therapist to Choose: A Water. A Water will pull the Woods into a world of creativity that will help the Woods unplug from their work world and see life in a new light.

FIRE AND FIRE

What fun! A Fire and a Fire will often find themselves center stage, laughing, playing, and making everyone around them happy. However, while these two are wearing feather boas and drinking martinis, the laundry, dishes, and business plans will be piling up. Daily tasks don't get done on their own, and the mountain of unattended business will continue to grow. While this thought usually makes the Fire couple laugh, laughter won't help them get out of their all-fun, no-reality imbalance. Plus, these two may just burn each other out or make each other anxious if they have been together too long. Fires are lit from the inside and tend to live on the surface, so many times they would like the depth of a person like a Water.

The Friend in Need or the Therapist to Choose: A Wood. A Wood's no-nonsense approach and dry sense of humor can pull the Fires back to reality without making them feel doused. Things can get done with everyone still having fun.

EARTH AND EARTH

An Earth and an Earth will love each other deeply. These two people come from the heart in everything they do. They will nurture, comfort, and take care of each other; the relationship may feel like the one they've always longed for, giving them the feeling of safety with family. The downside is that they may be so much inside their love space that they overlook practical life. They will realize that doing things together is not the same as getting things done.

The Friend in Need or the Therapist to Choose: A Fire. A Fire will respect the love that is in the air between two Earths but will also have the energy to motivate the Earths to come back to reality.

METAL AND METAL

Two Metals will hold each other in high esteem. When they walk into the room, they might seem like the queen and king of England. Theirs is a relationship of excellence, honor, and respect. However, they will need to keep spontaneity, passion, and joy on their radar or risk sitting around elegantly having tea and reading the paper all day instead of really engaging. Then again, they might be OK with that.

The Friend in Need or the Therapist to Choose: An Earth. An Earth can be the bridge of gentle joy for Metals to feel connected through warmth, which can foster spontaneity and passion.

Yin and Yang

You are probably familiar with the yin-yang symbol. It became popular with surfers and hippies in the seventies and has been a frequently used icon ever since. Yin and yang characters are ancient, found in inscriptions made on animal bones used in ancient Chinese divination practices as early as the fourteenth century B.C.E.

In simple terms, everything on earth has a yin tendency or a yang tendency. Yin is inner directed, soft, gentle, flowing, yielding, passive, diffused, cold, and wet; it is associated with water, earth, the moon, femininity, and night. Yang is outer directed, fast, hard, solid, focused, sharp, hot, dry, and aggressive; it is associated with fire, the sky, the sun, masculinity, and daytime.

Yin and yang principles apply to human beings and also to the Five Elements. In traditional Chinese medicine, good health is directly related to the balance between yin and yang properties and how they flow through the body's meridian system, which is an energy pathway in the body.

Within your primary element (Water, Wood, Fire, Earth, or Metal), you can be more yin or more yang, and be ruled more by one organ than another. For instance, a Wood person can be either a yin Wood or a yang Wood. I am a yin Wood, so I won't be as aggressive or as tough as a yang Wood can be. Furthermore, the liver will have more impact in my life than the gallbladder; both are Wood organs, but the liver is yin and the gallbladder is yang.

To put it simply, yang elements are more obvious and assertive with their main emotion, whatever it is—fear, anger, joy, compassion, or grief. Yin elements will be subtler, more subdued, and more gentle in expressing themselves.

Circadian Rhythms and Body Cycles

Pages 242 and 243 list some basic differences between yin and yang elements, along with the associated organ and times of the day when the qualities of this organ are most active. These times of day pertain to the way energies flow in the body in a twenty-four-hour cycle. You may have heard of circadian rhythms, which are physical, mental, and behavioral changes that follow a roughly twenty-four-hour cycle. These rhythms are found in human beings, animals, plants, and even microbes. The first account of circadian rhythms—an observation of the daily movement of tamarind leaves—was recorded in the fourth century B.C.E. by Androsthenes of Thasos, one of Alexander the Great's admirals. These daily rhythms affect all living things, and they have a direct connection to your elemental makeup.

For instance, many people are used to having an energy slump in the afternoon. In the Five Elements system, one to three P.M. every day is "bladder time," when the bladder is most active and when many people's energies decline. It is true that some might have had a meal that taxes their bladder energy. Continual oversweetened and oversalted, high-carbohydrate meals (specifically overloaded with common table salt, which lacks the essential minerals of sea salt) cause leptin resistance, making the brain unable to sense when the body has had enough food. There can also be insulin resistance, making the body unable to access energy stored as fat and so forcing it to lurch from one glucose rush to the next, with a hypoglycemic crash in between. Some might simply be Waters, who are governed by the bladder. But a big meal isn't always to blame—the afternoon low energy of "bladder time" can come up for anyone, whether they had a big lunch or not. It is wise to remember that the bladder is associated with Water, an element that must have downtime to be productive and energized.

This afternoon slump doesn't affect only Waters. It is the natural time to rest and restore. Energy actually declines a bit, and many cultures honor this time of restoration. Many people take naps in the afternoon. Some workplaces even allow siestas after lunch. In the United States, no business would dream of closing its doors for a couple of hours in the middle of the day. We prefer to fight through the fatigue with caffeine and sugary, fatty snacks.

On the other side of the daily cycle, one to three A.M. is "liver time." The liver is associated with Wood, and many Wood people are productive at night, getting an extra jolt of energy in the hours leading up to one A.M. These "night owls" prefer to go to bed late and sleep in past the morning hours, when others are starting their day.

Is there a time of day when you notice an energy slump or surge? Even if you don't notice anything different in your energy during the specific times of the day listed, for better or for worse, the elements and organs *are* being affected. This is why I never believe articles and books that say that the most successful people go to bed early and get up early. Sure, maybe they're the first ones in the office or they have an hour to get things done before waking the kids, but it doesn't mean they're successful or in their most productive and healthiest rhythm. There are some people who will never feel good going to bed early, waking up early, or exercising early, yet Western society insists that the same schedule works for everyone. Some people have very different rhythms; to be successful, they pay attention to those times of the day when their energy ebbs and flows. There is a reason why Metals like India, Earths and Waters resonate with the flowing vibe of places like Jamaica and other tropical islands, Fires like any spot with fun activity, and a lot of Woods are in New York City. The rhythm of these places feed them!

Understanding how yin and yang affect our health can give us helpful insights into our long-term wellness and longevity. One of my favorite books on the subject is *Between Heaven and Earth: A Guide to Chinese Medicine,* by Harriet Beinfield and Efrem Korngold. If you'd like to learn more, this is an excellent resource.

241

Are You a Yin or a Yang Element?

Your Element Is Water

YANG WATER:

- Associated with the bladder.
- Yang Waters need to play often.
- "Bladder time" is three to five P.M.

YIN WATER:

- Associated with the kidneys.
- Yin Waters need to rest often.
- "Kidney time" is five to seven P.M.

Your Element Is Wood

YANG WOOD:

- Associated with the gallbladder.
- Yang Woods need to express anger.
- "Gallbladder time" is eleven P.M. to one A.M.

YIN WOOD:

- Associated with the liver.
- Yin Woods need to be heard and acknowledged.
- "Liver time" is one to three A.M.

Your Element Is Fire

YANG FIRE:

- Associated with the small intestine and triple warmer (our fight-or-flight response).
- Yang Fires are swinging from the chandeliers.
- "Small intestine time" is one to three P.M., and "triple warmer time" is nine to eleven P.M.

YIN FIRE:

- Associated with the heart and the pericardium.
- Yin Fires smile, laugh, and love openly.
- "Heart time" is eleven A.M. to one P.M., and "pericardium time" is seven to nine P.M.

Your Element Is Earth

YANG EARTH:

- Associated with the stomach.
- Yang Earths can overprotect.
- "Stomach time" is seven to nine A.M.

YIN EARTH:

- Associated with the spleen.
- Yin Earths bring compassion.
- "Spleen time" is nine to eleven A.M.

Your Element Is Metal

YANG METAL:

- Associated with the large intestine.
- Yang Metals are in service to people until the job is done.
- "Large intestine time" is five to seven A.M.

YIN METAL:

- Associated with the lungs.
- Yin Metals provide structure.
- "Lung time" is three to five A.M.

The Five Elements Wheel

In Chinese medicine, the Five Elements are arranged in the form of a wheel. It's like the wheel of life, each element symbolizing a phase and an energetic quality of life. It starts with Water, which represents winter and the embryonic time when we hibernate. The second element is Wood, which represents spring, when we're bursting forth with new energy. Third is Fire, representing summer and a warm, joyful freedom. Earth is fourth, representing the tran-

243

sitions between seasons, the equinoxes and solstices. The last element in the wheel is Metal, which represents fall, the end of the cycle.

The organs on the outside of the wheel are the yang organs; those on the inside are the yin organs.

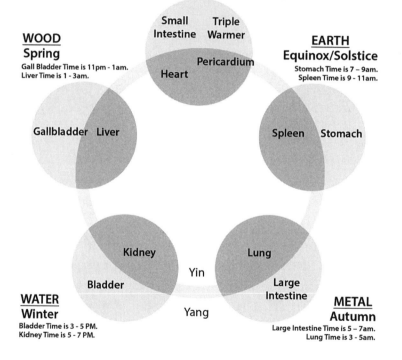

FIRE
Summer
Small Intestine Time is 1 – 3pm and Triple Warmer Time is 9 – 11pm.
Heart Time is 11am – 1pm and Pericardium Time 7 – 9pm.

WOOD
Spring
Gall Bladder Time is 11pm - 1am.
Liver Time is 1 - 3am.

EARTH
Equinox/Solstice
Stomach Time is 7 – 9am.
Spleen Time is 9 - 11am.

Small Intestine   Triple Warmer
Heart   Pericardium

Gallbladder   Liver

Spleen   Stomach

Kidney
Bladder

Yin

Lung
Large Intestine

Yang

WATER
Winter
Bladder Time is 3 - 5 PM.
Kidney Time is 5 - 7 PM.

METAL
Autumn
Large Intestine Time is 5 – 7am.
Lung Time is 3 - 5am.

The Five Elements for Children

Tips for Parents, Teachers, and Caregivers

by Titanya Dahlin

■

WOULDN'T IT BE GREAT if one handbook explained how to satisfy, communicate with, calm, and guide the children we're raising? We could give this precious book to grandparents, babysitters, and even teachers to help explain our kids. However, children's natures never follow every aspect of any handbook, no matter which expert writes it. Children have their own unique personalities, upbringings, and environmental influences; even within one family, children can be very different from one another. One child might be very outgoing and competitive, with high self-esteem, while another might be reclusive, preferring to be quiet and alone in his or her activities. Today there are even more unique children being born than ever before, all with individual talents and intuitive gifts. One way to understand who they are and to meet their needs is by understanding their unique personalities in the context of the Five Elements. Once you tune in to children's elements, you can begin to predict their behaviors and create new techniques to help balance stressful moments. You may even get clues about their primary elements simply by witnessing their moments of joy or stress. Honoring their uniqueness helps you to support and love them rather than feeling as if you're in a constant battle with them. This in turn helps them to blossom into the person they are meant to be, allowing them to meet life's challenges better, in school, at home, and in social situations. When you relate the aspects of the Five Elements to your children's personalities, you can help strengthen the family relationships.

The Five Elements in children look different than they do in adults. Children are exploring the world for the first time. They really have no emotional filters, social concepts, or norms of how to behave. Little kids especially can experience a roller coaster of emotions in a single day, so the elements may appear exaggerated at times. Parents may not know that young children go through the Five Elements many times every day; in contrast, adults stay in their primary element most of the time. It may be difficult to spot a child's primary element if he or she is younger than seven years old; before that age, kids are still cycling through all of the elements to find their own. After their seventh year, children begin to ground themselves in their primary element, and then their secondary and tertiary elements also start to appear. Occasionally, a child's primary element can shift as a result of a traumatic experience. This is more common during the preteen-to-puberty years.

In the first years of life, children are looking for guidance and trying to understand the world from the examples and teachings around them. Sensitive to their environment, as well people's emotions and behaviors, children are constantly picking up energy without even knowing it. Children today are highly evolved in spirituality, intuition, and wisdom, making them even more closely attuned to their surroundings. When you view the Five Elements from a child's points of view, you may begin to learn more about yourself and even connect to a part of yourself that may have been forgotten. Adults commonly have unresolved issues. When we get hurt, we may go right back to those difficult feelings from childhood. Being a parent can put you in positions that challenge you to identify your own emotional triggers and wounds. By understanding your own childhood experiences through knowing each of the Five Elements and what elements the people were in your life growing up (with their strengths and challenges), you may start to resolve wounds that cause you emotional pain as an adult.

When children learn about the beauty and challenges within their own elements, they too can establish a grounded sense of confidence and self-worth. They can also learn about members of the family through each person's elemental style. This helps everyone learn to respect one another and understand what's required to weave a harmonious dance together as a family.

Children are wide open to learn. In their hearts, minds, and energy fields, they have a lot of trust in their caregivers, including their teachers. Teachers can have a positive impact on children, helping them to reach their fullest potential, or they can have a negative impact, perhaps without even knowing it. Many times when I have gone into schools, I have seen that the teacher is energetically off or having a bad day. This imbalance creates learning challenges for the children in the class. Once the teacher's energies are balanced, the children can focus, listen, and learn more easily. Helping your children to understand their own elements can help them notice when their energy is imbalanced—or when someone else's is. In this chapter, I offer Eden Energy Medicine to balance all of the Five Elements in kids. They're great activities for a family or a classroom to practice together. We all need to balance our energies!

The Water Child

Winter's Child Is Water

Mariah was a very shy girl who kept to herself on the playground as she watched the other girls playing. She felt excluded and alone, so she'd make up her own fantasy games and imaginary friends, yet she secretly wanted a real friend. At home, she spent a lot of time swimming in the family pool with all of her imaginary mermaid friends. Mariah had a pudgy little body that still held on to her baby fat even as she grew older.

Sometimes Mariah would get picked on for being too weird. In class, she never wanted the teacher to call on her, for fear of sticking out. Instead, she slumped down in her chair whenever the teacher looked for an answer from the children. Even choosing a seat on the school bus was a huge dilemma. She felt that others didn't like her, so she began to pretend to be sick just so she wouldn't have to go to school, or she'd hide behind a tree to purposefully miss the bus. These fears and avoidances grew. (If not checked, these little fears and avoidances can grow and grow until they become big problems.)

Mariah was actually a good student. She loved to read and would devour many books in a week, moving on to the next exciting reading adventure as soon as she was done with the last one. However, at parent-teacher conferences, Mariah's parents couldn't understand why they were told that their daughter was reclusive and distant from the rest of the class. Her teacher was concerned. It was true that when she got home, she ran to her bedroom to feel safe again. Generally, though, at home she was a great storyteller with a wild

248

imagination; she expressed herself outwardly. She was always starting new creative projects and couldn't wait to tell her parents about what she was going to do, even if the enthusiasm and momentum were always gone before the projects were finished.

Mariah began to feel unseen when her baby sister came along. She felt that her parents were not giving her attention anymore. When they didn't seem to understand her feelings of separateness, Mariah became more withdrawn and unreachable. She began to seethe with jealousy, thinking, *Well, if I ran away from home, no one would ever really miss me.*

Mariah's mom began to notice her daughter's withdrawal. One day she asked if Mariah wanted to have her very own "mommy-daughter time" in the kitchen a few afternoons a week. They could make lunch while the baby took her naps. With a sigh of relief, a big smile came over Mariah's face and she hugged her mommy.

Just like the little mermaid in Hans Christian Andersen's story of the same name, Waters live beneath the surface in a world of fantasy. As the mermaid dreamed of joining the land of the two-legged humans, Waters dream of joining in the play with other girls and boys. Water children are trying to find their own powerful voices, like the little mermaid herself. They are wise when they do speak but timid until they do. Water babies may develop more slowly and speak later in life as well. Encouragement and compassionate understanding of their own timely process helps Water children blossom with their courageous voices.

Water is first in the Five Elements cycle. It is the season of Winter. Water kids hibernate into their own feelings and worlds. While the surface of the earth is still and frozen, there's a lot germinating under the surface, getting ready for

249

spring. Similarly, Water children may sometimes see things that are not there, such as classmates talking about them or parents who think they are nuisances. Water teenagers may go so deep into their inner world that parents may not know what's really going on with them. If Water children or teens feel rejected or make mistakes, they will withdraw even more, making it even harder to reach them. They need to feel acknowledged—that they belong and that their ideas matter. They want to be understood and have people see them for who they really are.

Fear is Water's ruling emotion. It can grow so huge within that it may become a source of ongoing depression. Water children can be very shy. They keep to themselves and sometimes have very few friends, although they will be deeply connected to the friends they do have.

Water children can have pudgy bodies because they hold on to water within their cells. Still, they need to drink more water in order to flow more within their energies. Drinking water will allow more circulation in their joints and better emotional movement to happen rather than feeling stuck in their sensitivities, unable to find a way out. Movements like swimming and dance help them move their stuck energies, ease their minds, and connect to their creativity.

Water children will have incredible imaginations and will tend to make up entertaining stories. Because they live in their own fantasy worlds, they might even have unseen friends. (Listen to them when they tell you about their interesting ideas or imaginary companions.) Elusive Water children can harbor secrets. They live in a conundrum: They don't want anyone knowing who they really are, and yet they really want people to understand them. It can be difficult to get to know them because of this internal conflict. As teenagers, they may be interested in goth culture, esoteric subjects, and dark mysteries.

Water children can be very excited to start a new project but may not follow it through completely. They like new things, such a new friend or a new hobby, and yet they may need more inspiration and time than others to develop the friendship or the interest. They will give up early on projects if they feel insecure or are criticized. They may not complete homework or practice a musical instrument consistently, which can be very frustrating to parents trying to help keep them on track. Water kids will be lost in their work long after the project needs to be finished and other students have moved on. Time and deadlines, like homework, can be difficult for them.

If you allow them their own processes, they will eventually meander into the perfect rhythm for themselves. Positive encouragement will bring out their best work. Don't force your own plans on them. Refrain from berating them about not finishing but instead help support them to create better plans for themselves around schoolwork. Water children will respect that you're trying to meet them in this way.

This gentle approach helps them to recognize their own Water rhythm and pace themselves within it. Waters can be brilliant artists, musicians, or poets, and they will spend most of their time in these pursuits, allowing their inner expression to be heard. Art and music are usually their favorite subjects in school. Give them an outlet for this form of expression. Water kids also love to read and usually have many books. They can be curious about people and how things work.

In school, they will have the answers in class but may not speak out for fear of attracting too much attention. Teachers need to pay special attention to Water children for this reason. They are afraid of being embarrassed, of standing out and being made fun of. They feel comfortable in smaller groups. Because Water

251

children are searching for meaning, they can ask many questions and talk a lot when they feel safe. Water kids may feel all alone in a world that's out to get them. They can be vulnerable to bullies, and when they experience low self-esteem, they find it hard to come back to a sense of empowerment.

Water children can be very sensitive to the environment around them, so their emotions can change quickly and unexpectedly. A wonderful day can sometimes go bad when imbalanced Water children bring up their insecurities. They can be crybabies and have a "poor me" attitude, drawing all the attention to them and their needs, not realizing that they are being self-centered. Being misunderstood is a constant threat for Water children. If words are difficult, help them express themselves in images or colors. When they are balanced, Waters go with the flow and are extremely creative, wise, and helpful.

How to Help Your Water Child

- ♥ **Motivate them by inspiring their own creativity.** Waters have deep creative minds, so encourage them to come up with their own ideas. Buy them art sets to help express themselves through color, especially if they don't talk a lot. Create manifestation boards, especially during times of low self-esteem or when they begin new projects. When they're old enough, encourage them to write down their thoughts in a notebook or journal.

- ♥ **Give them a quiet place where they can create their very own sanctuary.** Creating a personal space, such as an altar table or a treehouse, gives Water children a place of safety. Inspire them to fill it with their favorite things. To help them meet their personal goals, encourage them to change their altar table or manifestation board frequently as their lives change.

♥ **Help them to stay motivated.** Waters need a lot of praise to establish a powerful sense of self-worth and to stay on track. They need to feel that you are there for them like a life raft, even if they may not reach for you. Fear of the unknown is their biggest enemy. It is important for Water kids to feel safe.

♥ **Establish routines for family time.** Create dinnertime schedules and make the meal a place for the family to share the day's stories rather than an excuse to retreat to separate corners or behind an iPad, cell phone, or a television set. This will bring Water children out of their shells and establish a stronger family connection.

♥ **Give them special roles for helping out.** Help them know their place in the family. A new baby can make them retreat, imagining that they are just in the way. Water kids can feel that they are not seen, heard, or understood. Remind them that they aren't invisible. Give them fun things to do to help out with the new baby or new situation. Create special times for just them alone.

♥ **Acknowledge them.** In classroom situations, make sure they are heard and seen, not left out. Partner them with other Water kids or with Fire kids to bring them out of their shells. Water kids can get overwhelmed in big groups. Create smaller groups in which

253

they feel more comfortable. Listen to them; they have a wealth of wisdom to teach you.

- ♥ **Be aware of your voice and body language.** Water children are very sensitive, especially with their ears. Be aware of the tone of your voice and your body expression. Harsh tones may make Water children clam up even more, and then they won't hear you anyway.

- ♥ **Help them to find their own voice.** Water kids don't talk very much. Sometimes their habit of being silent can make it hard to find the words to express themselves. Create safety for them to talk.

- ♥ **Swimming.** Water kids can come alive when they have some sort of outlet to help them flow with their energy. Swimming lessons or water sports will do wonders for their lethargic energy and give them a sense of pride. Even putting a small fountain in the house would be good for them. Running water brings a sense of flow to the Water child.

254

The Water Child Overview

Water Child Archetypes	The Creative Artist, the Wise Child
Animal Archetype	Turtle (hides away within protective shell)
Water's Superpowers	Water children are very wise and can go very deep if you listen to them. They have great imaginations, and they can tell great stories. They are very creative artistically and musically, and in balance, they are honest and kind.
Water's Fears	Fear is a huge issue with Water children. They can be suspicious of parents, teachers, and even friends. They most want to avoid exposure, embarrassment, and shame. They may lie if they feel threatened. These children get picked on, as they don't know how to stick up for themselves. They have unexplainable fears and confusion.
Water's Challenges	When they get hurt, they can detach from people and be hard to reach. They go into depression and can't find a way out. Having a pet around helps "Water babies" with depression.
Stress Responses	Waters get hurt easily, retreat, and internalize illusions. They detach and can go into deep depression. They may not hear you when overwhelmed. Think of the Eeyore character. Water kids may groan, cry, and whine until they get their way.

(continued)

255

Water's Needs	Water children need to feel understood. Find a way to help them talk about what's bothering them rather than hiding it away, but don't meddle too much, as it will make them withdraw more. Let them know you're there. Hugs are great if nothing else works.
	Instill inspiration and hope in them.
	They need to find their tribe.
Physical Reactions	Frequent urination, swayback, scoliosis, water retention, adrenal stress, dark circles under eyes, teeth issues, ear sensitivity, lethargy, lower back pain.
Water's Lessons	Waters need to believe, trust, and build self-esteem.
	Instill faith and courage within them every day.
	When they feel all alone, they need to let others help them.
The Water Parent	The Philosopher. They want to go deep with their children, counseling kids along the way. Trust the process and let go of fears.
Water Movement	Water kids need more flow in their bodies. Tai Chi, swimming.
Water Exercise	Dolphin leap

Water Exercise: Dolphin Leap

Most Water children who are shy have energy fields that are pulled close to their bodies. This makes them more susceptible to having their energy thrown off even by the slightest thing. Dolphin Leap puffs up and strengthens the aura so that they aren't as sensitive. It also helps the energy cross over from the right to left fields to help them focus, come out of depression, and find more joy.

| FIG. 1 | FIG. 2 | FIG. 3 |

1. Cross your wrists and clasp your hands into a pretzel pose (Figs. 1, 2, 3).
2. Breathe in and pull your body up.
3. Breathe out with the sound of the wind, "Whooo . . . ," bend over like a wave, and envision your problems blowing away (Fig. 3).

FIG. 4   **FIG. 5**

4. Breathe in again and pull your body back up to the sunlight (Fig. 4).

5. Do this three times. The third time, pretend you're a dolphin jumping out of the water. Open up your hands and arms in a beautiful breaststroke to each side (Fig. 5).

Ideas for the Classroom. Dance with colorful scarves or veils, pretending to be flowing under Water, like seaweed. Pretend to be mer-people, swimming deep in the blue sea. What fish do you see there? Jump out of the Water and emerge to see the light above. Use the sound of "Whooo" while dancing to the sounds of the ocean wind. Tchaikovsky's *Swan Lake* is the perfect background music.

258

The Wood Child

Spring's Child Is Wood

Luke was a Wood child in every aspect of his being. He marched into the room in his karate uniform as if he had a chip on his shoulder. Luke held out his awards for his parents to see, bragging about how he won the match.

"Good going, Luke!" His father said.

"Yep, I won. I was the best there! Oliver had nothing on me!" Luke boasted as he showed them a few of his moves. His father quickly pulled Luke's baby brother out of the way from an incoming karate chop and kick.

"Luke, watch where you're kicking!" his father exclaimed.

Luke's mother was always proud of him but began to explain to him that he was getting a very big ego from his successes. She told him to put up his awards and get on with his homework before dinner. Luke began to talk back to his mom with attitude, saying he really didn't need to study anymore because he was going to be a big martial arts stuntman for the movies anyway, like Jet Li or Jackie Chan. He stomped away to his room with a defiant, stubborn attitude, pushing his baby brother out of the way.

"You need to calm down and tame that inner dragon before you come down for dinner," Luke's mom said.

Like the leaves that sprout from spring trees, Wood children burst forth with an attitude that says, "I'm here! Pay attention to me." They want parents and teachers to listen to their ideas, but they will also challenge authority and push boundaries. They have an assertiveness behind what they say. They can be real show-offs.

Wood kids like to take risks, such as climbing trees and jumping off of things. Their bodies are sturdy and reliable, grounded, square shaped, and solid. Nothing can knock them over. They are built for sports, which they usually enter into later on, especially in high school. Wood kids love competitions of any kind and are usually the captains of school teams and clubs. They can be very critical of themselves if they make a mistake or lose, but instead of lowering their self-esteem, a setback drives them to greater accomplishments. They compete with themselves as much as with anyone else.

Empowered Wood children push boundaries to see how far they can go with the adults around them. As teenagers, they may do this even more. They love to debate their point of view and many times can end up in an argumentative conflict when others don't see their brilliant perspective. Think of a bulldog's energy. Woods always seem ready for a challenge or a quick reply. They like to be unique and express what's on their mind. If their creative freedom is restricted, they can become hostile. When things don't go according to plan, they may get very frustrated and act out in destructive ways.

When Woods are young, they can be very physical. When hormones run high in the teen years, Wood kids, whose ruling emotion is anger, may break things or take out their frustration on other people. Make them aware of the relationship between behaviors and consequences early on. Wood kids can become bullies if they feel small. To feel better, they may pick on others. Although sometimes intimidating, Wood children can actually be very nice. When balanced, they stick up for underdogs and can befriend those in need. They protect their friends and even get aggressive if they see their friends hurt.

260

Woods are little entrepreneurs who move forward confidently in their ideas. They create the necessary detailed plans to reach their goals. They are leaders and will direct every step of the way, escorting their family and friends into the proper roles to fulfill their needs. Make sure you praise them, their homework, or their accomplishments, for they take real pride in reaching goals. Wood kids are hard workers and can have good homework habits when they put their minds to it. Their elemental time is at night; they tend to come alive from eleven P.M. to three A.M., so it's hard to get them to sleep on school nights and prevent them from sleeping in on school days.

If they are required to do something, it had better make sense to them. Wood kids look for the truth, and they know when you're lying to them. If you give them a time-out, make sure you also give a good reason for it, as well as something for them to do. Wood kids need to let off some steam; otherwise, their anger has no place to go. If allowed to seethe inside, it will come out at another time and be even worse. Having them do an energy exercise or punch pillows rather than someone or something else, can help calm them. Later, you can talk with them about which exercise they chose and why, creating a dialogue to address the stressful situation.

Parents, caretakers, and teachers must understand that saying no to Wood children without a good reason will not gain their respect. They will likely get angrier and throw a fit. Try to communicate more, rather than just yelling and repeating yourself. Talk with them in a calm and clear manner, and be relaxed in your body language. This will naturally bring down their own stress responses. Find ways to praise them first, and then show them where they may have been wrong. Help them to create their own solutions to the problem. This will help them to develop awareness and keep them out of black-and-white thinking. When Woods become adults, this black-and-white thinking can harden them and it can be difficult to soften again.

How to Help Your Wood Child

- ♥ **Give them responsibilities, with guidance.** Wood kids want to be the leaders and in control. They have good ideas, so give them proper jobs to support this trait. Make them feel special and learn responsibility, but also give them guidelines so they don't go overboard, which is easy for them to do.

- ♥ **Acknowledge their performance strengths.** Woods love to win and hate to lose, so if they do lose, help them to make new goals and feel better about themselves. Help them to understand the other players' sensitivities as well.

- ♥ **Introduce them to other cultures and social differences.** Wood children can be very self-focused. Introduce them and all of your children to as many cultures and ways of life as you can. This will broaden their horizons and help them to be more tolerant toward others as they grow up.

- ♥ **Help them to say "I'm sorry."** This is a hard one for Woods in general. They can be very judgmental and say whatever is on their mind. Later on, however, they'll usually regret their frank and sometimes unfeeling words but they may not know how to say, "I'm sorry."

262

- ♥ **Reward Wood children.** They love to see where they've come from, where they're at, and where they're going. At home or at school, give them accomplishment posters, stickers, and rewards. Rewards for good behavior will be more effective than punishment for bad.

- ♥ **Find them a mentor.** If you cannot reach Wood children yourself, find someone whom they can look up to. Often someone outside the family, having more distance, has an easier time gaining Wood children's respect.

- ♥ **Harness their anger.** Give them a physical outlet for their anger, such as playing a drum kit or practicing martial arts. Drums can be a very healing tool and can help release the Wood kids' frustrated energies. Martial arts are strict, sacred disciplines taught by a sensei (teacher). The practice can help children control emotions and respect themselves while offering them healthy competition. Martial arts will help all of their relationships now, and as they grow into young adults.

The Wood Child Overview

Wood Child Archetypes	The Warrior, the Director
Animal Archetype	Bulldog (sturdy, strong, and ready for anything)
Wood's Superpowers	Woods will stick up for their friends. They can be very nice, considerate, and helpful when balanced.
Wood's Fears	Woods fear losing face or losing the game. They don't like making mistakes or being out of control.
Wood's Challenges	Tunnel vision. Woods will think they are right most of the time, even above authority. They can show a lack of sensitivity for other children. They have a hard time forgiving.
Stress Responses	Woods get angry, and as children they will shout. They sometimes can lash out and attack whomever or whatever is in front of them. If their anger isn't addressed, they can seethe inside and blow up in destructive ways.
Wood's Needs	Woods need boundaries with good reasons for obeying parents and caregivers. They need to feel true praise from authority figures for their accomplishments.
Physical Reactions	Migraines, constipation, stiff or weak joints, eye problems, vertigo, muscle spasms.

Wood's Lessons	Practice releasing anger instead of exploding and then feeling deep regret. Practice accepting people who are different. Practice forgiveness and genuine apologies.
The Wood Parent	The Police Parent. Coaching their kids, they establish firm ground rules and boundaries. But be flexible; don't push too much. Watch that your body language and tone of voice don't get overbearing.
Wood Movement	Kicking and karate-chop movements. Wood children also need to stretch their bodies. Yoga can be good for them.
Wood Exercise	Tame Your Dragon.

Wood Exercise: Tame Your Dragon

Anger is the emotion for Wood. It is very important to get this anger out of the body, not stuff it inside. Have the Wood child bring to mind a source of anger or frustration or anything she needs to get rid of.

FIG. 1 FIG. 2 FIG. 3

1. Start with fists. With a deep in-breath, swing your arms out to your sides as if you're raising your mighty dragon wings. Complete the circle by bringing them high above your head (Fig. 1).

2. Grab some "angry energy" with your dragon wings right above your head and hold it in your two fists (Fig. 2).

3. Like a powerful dragon with fire breath, make a loud "Rooooaaarrr!" as you exhale. Bring your fisted hands down fast, right in front of you, opening them at the bottom to get rid of this "icky angry energy." Give it to the earth. (Tell the child that the earth can always recycle our negative energy and turn it into

266

positive energy. It's not good to keep it inside you, because it can make your outlook more and more negative or even make you sick.

4. Do this three times. The third time, do it very slowly. When your hands get to the bottom, push out the last remaining angry energy from your throat and stick your tongue out as though it holds the last bit of poison from the dragon's throat, like this, "Haahhhhhhh . . ." (Fig. 3).

FIG. 4

FIG. 5

5. Bring your hands up the center of your body. When they get above your head, make a big heart around your body with your dragon wings of light. Bring in positive feelings (Fig. 4).

6. Close your wings around you and let your hands land in the middle of your chest or give yourself a nice big hug! Your dragon has now been tamed and is nice again (Fig. 5).

Ideas for the Classroom. When your class hits an afternoon slump, it could benefit from some Wood energy. Have children pretend to flick, kick, and throw away their anger or obstacles with sounds like "Shhhh!" or "Ha!" Pretend that your class is a tribe of dragons or dinosaurs riding through a big storm, removing obstacles. Music: Wagner's "Ride of the Valkyries."

The Fire Child

Summer's Child Is Fire

Kayleigh's vibrant personality was driven by her Fire nature. She burst into the room with a bright pink boa around her neck. She wore a purple sparkly princess dress with matching shoes, tiara, and scepter.

"Ta-da! Today's my birthday!" she announced, giving a dramatic twirl and curtsey. She was excited that all of her friends were coming over to celebrate at her very own fairy princess party. She loved parties and celebrations of all kinds and had planned the details of this one with her mom's help. The backyard was decorated with balloons and fairy lights. All of a sudden Kayleigh screamed, "Where are my fairy wings?" She couldn't find them, and it felt like the end of the world. Everything had been just perfect, but now everything was wrong.

"Calm down, Kayleigh. We'll find them," her mother said.

"No, we won't! We won't! We won't! We have to cancel the party if I can't find my fairy wings!" Tears began to stream down Kayleigh's face. The first of her guests began to arrive while she was in her bedroom freaking out. Luckily, the birthday clown was already making balloon animals to keep the guests happy as they arrived. All of her friends were going to have their fairy wings on but she—the birthday girl!—wouldn't have any. It wasn't fair!

Kayleigh cried hysterically and collapsed in a heap of pink feathers and purple sparkle. Her mother rocked her to calm her down before looking for the precious wings. They were behind a chair that was covered in costumes and

269

toys. Flinging them on with excited glee, Kayleigh went flying into her birthday party, celebrating as if nothing had ever gone wrong.

Fire children express outwardly, love to play outdoors in the playground or at the beach, and hate to be cooped up inside. The sun is out and they're on the go! They're like fireworks.

Wild Fire children love celebrations of any kind, especially if they are the ones being celebrated. They love make-believe too, and wearing colorful, crazy clothing. Halloween can be an exciting time for them.

Fire children love to laugh and are naturally funny themselves. They usually have a giggle in their speech. They talk with their hands, and their experiences can be exaggerated in the most dramatic ways. Some Fire kids need to learn about spatial awareness, for when they get excited, their energy expands and their expressive hands and body may knock things over or hit people.

Fire kids love to be the center of attention and may appear self-centered, wanting all of your attention at the worst possible moments. They may also be show-offs and class clowns, acting out spontaneously. Sometimes in their joy, Fire children blurt something out that's on their mind. They don't mean to hurt others; they simply need to slow down and think before making decisions or speaking. With so much charisma, they can also convince fellow classmates to follow them in playing pranks.

Fire children have huge, vibrant personalities and can be very popular in school, with lots of friends. They also love to flirt. Every week they may be talking about a new "puppy love" crush. When young, they're your best little friends, loving to talk and share their daily dramas with you. Once they hit the preteen years, they may choose to share with their friends instead. The Fire element is the time of the teenager. Teach them from an early age about healthy boundaries and appropriate sexual behavior. It's the Fire kids who succumb to peer pressure or their own pleasure-seeking curiosity and upend their lives by getting into trouble with sex. Let them know you're there and give them gentle boundaries embraced by love. Be patient; this season will pass. Fire teens will come back around in time. Fires are very physical, so hugs are a good option if talking isn't working.

Fire kids have short attention spans in class and difficulty retaining information, especially if it doesn't interest them. They crave stimulation all the time and hate being bored. These are the kids who are often labeled ADD or ADHD, but in reality they may just have a lot of Fire. Subjects need to come alive for them with lots of colorful visuals and activities. Once engaged, they are excellent and interested students.

These kids can be unpredictable in their emotions. Like Fire, they shift their energies with the moment. Make sure sugar is limited in their diet. The American Heart Association recommends no more than three added teaspoons of sugar a day for children aged four to eight. More sugar than this can catapult already dramatic children into craziness and hyperactivity, creating unnecessary stress and embarrassment for themselves and others.

Children's brains function different than adults' do, especially during huge emotional traumas. Many adults try to reason with their children. During stressful times, there is so much going on inside your Fire child that tuning in to an adult while she's in tears is very difficult for him. Wait until the acute situation has subsided before speaking with Fire children. When you do, make sure to use a calm and soothing manner. Under pressure, Fire children may stutter or grope for words. Be patient while you help them express themselves

271

and recognize their feelings. Their minds and emotions work so fast that their words often lag behind.

Because they lead from feelings of joy rather than logic, Fires may forget what they have promised or said days before. Adults also need to be patient with Fire children.

Decisions too can be difficult for Fires. A happy moment can turn into extreme drama for you or the child when the child is faced with a sudden, challenging decision. If too many things are coming at them all at once, Fires can easily be confused. Teach them discernment from a young age so that by the teen years, they'll be able to face the many choices and pressures of young adulthood without getting overwhelmed.

Fires can have messy rooms and grow up to be very disorganized in their environment and work. A messy room with lots of stuff can make a child hyper, uncontrollable, and sometimes even unhealthy. Put on some good music and help them clean up. Get them interested in feng shui, the ancient art of balancing the yin and yang elements in one's surroundings to create peace and harmony. Working with you, they will be able to create more calm and peace in the family home.

One of the best things about Fire kids is that they make everyday reality an animated experience of joy and magic. Their charismatic Fire spirits will enliven your routine. They live to celebrate the fun, exhilarating moments in life and will keep you on your toes and feeling young if you follow their lead.

272

How to Help Your Fire Child

♥ **Keep a daily routine.** Keep similar schedules from day to day. Fire kids love spontaneity if it's a fun surprise, but if it's an unplanned event, they may become unbalanced and act out in public. They need time to prepare for changes, because they're always so engrossed in their experiences. Countdowns are good, but allow a good amount of time for them to adjust when you say it's time to go.

♥ **Keep your promises.** Fire kids build up expectations when you make a promise or a plan. Beware of promises not kept; they will remember broken promises.

♥ **Balance their social activities with rest.** Fire kids resonate with high energy events. Make sure they get enough rest to balance their activities.

♥ **Wind them down early before bedtime.** Fire kids can be so wound up from the day's excitement that sleep doesn't come easily. On the other hand, they might be so overstimulated that they crash into bed. Either way, start to calm them down early in the evening. Paint their rooms shades of light blue for calm, tranquility, and sleep.

♥ **Let them be a part of planning celebrations and parties.** Fire children enjoy this sense of responsibility and may feel pride as they accomplish special tasks.

273

- ♥ **Give them time for decisions.** It's hard for Fire kids to make decisions. Let them sleep on their choices and act the following day. If they decide in the moment, they may choose something they don't really want. Be aware that Fire kids have a tendency to change their minds at the last second.

- ♥ **Empower them to resist peer pressure.** Fires can be influenced by others and may be easily manipulated. Help them see the bigger picture of situations instead of being swayed by the fun of the moment.

- ♥ **Help them to focus.** Set clear goals with them. Create a visual summary that highlights their accomplishments and shows their goals. Regarding homework, encourage them to take breaks every now and then. An energy exercise or dancing can keep them alert and focused.

- ♥ **Enroll them in a drama class.** Fire children love being onstage and have a knack for drama. Put it to good use! It will help empower them.

- ♥ **Help them to eat regularly.** Fires' metabolisms run quick and hot, and these kids may have a tendency toward hypoglycemia, mood swings, and overheating. Establish a regular meal schedule. Fires are so in-the-moment that they may forget to eat.

274

The Fire Child Overview

Fire Child Archetypes	The Free Spirit, the Class Clown, or the Social Butterfly
Animal Archetype	Monkey or Puppy (happy energy that goes everywhere and can't be controlled)
Fire's Superpowers	They believe in the good in everyone and bring joy to every moment.
Fire's Fears	They are scared that they won't have friends.
Fire's Challenges	They can take on too many things, get overwhelmed, and panic. Life is a soap opera all the time! They can exaggerate.
Stress Responses	They can scream and fall apart.
Fire's Needs	They want to be loved and needed. Make sure to give lots of unconditional love and appreciation.
Physical Reactions	Anxiety, nervousness, panic attacks, speech problems, sleeplessness, overheating, mood swings, hypersensitivity, circulation problems, fainting.

(continued)

275

Fire's Lessons	Fires need to breathe and pace themselves. They need to learn how to walk away from a situation before reacting suddenly.
The Fire Parent	The Party Parent. Every day is a celebration! They want to be their kids' best friends. Fire parents sometimes act like teenagers themselves, so this might make establishing boundaries for their kids difficult.
Fire Movement	Salsa, Zumba, and African dance
Fire Exercise	The Firefly

Fire Exercise: The Firefly

This exercise mirrors the child's emotion and rhythm in the moment and brings her back to a calm demeanor. It's a good one for winding down in the evening before bed.

FIG. 1

1. Create a fire with your hands and arms, shaking and vibrating them, and moving them about furiously as if they are flames. Make the flames play high and wild all around you, burning above your head. Pretend you're a fire! Dance wildly about the room! Wiggle about like a firefly lighting up the room. What sound does your firefly make? (Fig. 1).

277

| FIG. 2 | FIG. 3 | FIG. 4 | FIG. 5 |

2. When the fire has risen as high as it can go, let it burn out. Calm the fire down, right down to the ground. Bring one arm up above your head like your firefly wing and bring it down center line of your body (Figs. 2, 3).

3. Next, bring the other arm or firefly wing up above your head and bring that one all the way down the middle of your body (Figs. 4, 5).

4. Move your wings slowly up and down, bringing one arm down and then the other. Breathe calmly (Fig. 6).

FIG. 6   FIG. 7   FIG. 8

5. Now take that energy down your body with your hands traveling down the outside of your legs as you make the sound "Haaaaah. . . ." Keep going till you reach the ground. With your hands, give that crazy energy to the earth (Fig. 6, 7).

6. Now stand tall and strong and give yourself a hug (Fig. 8).

Ideas for the Classroom. If the class is getting too rowdy, you may need to match their energy and let them blow off some steam. Use wild, frenetic music, like Irish jigs. Then move into calming, peaceful music, coming back down to the ground to rest. Music: "Can-Can" by Offenbach.

The Earth Child

Equinox's Child Is Earth

"Sarah!" her mother called out the back door. "We need to go and you're not even dressed yet!"

Sarah came slowly ambling up the steps, barefoot and smiling, holding a bouquet of flowers. "Mom, I was just helping Grandma in the garden. Here, I brought you some freshly picked flowers!"

Sarah was a daydreamer, taking her time in whatever she was doing. "Sarah, thank you for the flowers, but your hands are filthy and we gotta go! Go wash up and get your good dress on. We're going to be late for parents' night!"

Sarah wasn't especially looking forward to showing her science project to a huge crowd on this night. It was far from complete; she'd been more interested in helping her friends finish *their* projects than in finishing her own. She was worried about getting a bad grade and didn't want to face the consequences. In her bedroom, instead of quickly getting dressed, she stalled for time. Her stomach began to churn, which usually happened when she worried.

"Mom, I don't feel well," Sarah groaned as she came down the stairs holding her tummy. Her mother, who had seen this behavior before, asked her daughter what was really going on. So Sarah told her about her concerns with the science project. Her mother took her in her arms and told her that, whatever happened, she knew Sarah had given it her best effort. Everything would turn out OK. Her mother hugged Sarah.

280

"I feel better now, Mom. Thank you. I love you." She jumped off of her mommy's knee, and they went off to parents' night together.

Equinoxes are times of transition and change. This is the time when the Earth element is in full balance. This is Indian summer, the lazy days lingering at the end of the hot season and before the cooler fall weather arrives. It is the beginning of harvest time, leading up to the thanksgivings, when we enjoy the fruits of our labors.

Earth children hold harmonious energy within them as they sway and walk with the rhythm of earth, always stopping to smell the flowers along the way. They are compassionate and caring, without bias. They make friends easily, love being part of a group, and treasure community and family. They befriend kids whom no one else will talk to; the ones who are either picked on, bullied, or cast out by others. Earth children see their true beauty. They can stick up for their friends, especially if they think they're being treated unfairly, but it's a lot harder for them to stick up for themselves. Caring Earth children forget to take care of their own needs.

They will genuinely be concerned if someone is hurt, sick, or feeling bad, and they will want to help take away the pain, even if they are too young or small to do so. They feel as if it is their own personal obligation to fix the problem. They are the children who send thank-you cards and get-well cards or take flowers to someone in need of comfort.

Like Waters, they live in fantasy worlds but are mostly focused on fairy-tale marriages and perfect family lives. They believe in fairy tales, handsome princes, beautiful princesses, and the happily-ever-after stories. Little Earth girls have baby dolls, while little Earth boys may have stuffed animals. Both

281

sexes care for their toys, which seem to be alive and have animated spirits living within them. On the playground, Earth girls play house, and sometimes Earth boys do too.

Homework can take a backseat in Earth's dreamy nature. When they put their minds to schoolwork, Earth kids can get it done; they just need to stay on track. When focused, Earth kids aim to please, especially if they love the subject or their teacher. They are willing to help out in class in any way they can. They can easily become the teacher's pet.

Earth children can embody the archetype of the good little girl or boy. Never wanting to rock the boat and always aiming to please the authority figures around them, they never complain. Earth children can be very accommodating to everyone's schedules. They are quiet most of the time and usually speak only when spoken to. Earth kids do not need to be the center of attention. They make room for everyone else to shine, but they are always trying to do their best and be acknowledged by their parents, caregivers, or teachers. They can be little chameleons, adjusting their energies and personalities to fit their environment and others around them. That said, they might tell white lies to save others from getting hurt. They may fib in order to protect a friendship or to avoid confrontation. The effort often fails, because Earth kids can look guilty even when they aren't.

Earth children are centered, peaceful, and calm. Because they need to find their own schedule with its own rhythm, they cannot be rushed into anything. Making a decision too quickly can be very upsetting. They don't like to confront or be confronted, so they will not face their problems right away. In fact, they may avoid admitting that there's a problem, as they have a tendency not to advertise when something is wrong. They are governed by the stomach and spleen, which metabolize food and emotional situations. As parents, you will want to look at the emotions when they complain of digestion issues.

Earth kids are not comfortable with change. When things change or come at them too quickly, they will become scattered and confused. Moving to a new home, adding a new member to the family, going through a divorce, or experiencing the death of a loved one can throw them off even more than these events affect others. Earth children do well by following the same schedules every day.

Your sweet Earth child loves to care for animals and will often bring home any stray or wounded one they find. Pets can help calm their depressed or confused energies, especially if they're experiencing a major transition or death in their lives. Caring for pets also teaches them about responsibilities.

Earth kids love to be outside in nature. On walks, they collect things like seashells, rocks, flowers, and bugs, making your outing a little longer than you may have wanted. Their bedrooms are often full of these collections. They may not do well living in a city where there is not a lot of nature to ground their energy. Urban Earth children will find solace in their homes and in parks.

Home and family are the most important things to Earth children. The first day of school can be a traumatic separation for them; similarly, they are often the last children to move out of the house as they approach adulthood. They dream of creating their own family someday but always stay close to their original families. When their households are harmonious, they too will be content. They will help you cook, garden, or fix a wound on one of their stuffed animals. Contented, they will be your best little helper. When their households are stressful, however, Earth children reflect this disharmony in their behaviors, schoolwork, and especially in their health and digestive systems.

283

Earth children's bodies are round or chubby, and they tend to keep their baby fat longer than others. They have a hard time metabolizing food and emotions, especially when their environment is stressful. Stress or unbalanced energy can get stuck in their bodies. They love sweets more than children of the other elements and this will probably last their whole lives. Watch their sugar intake, as they are prone to both hypoglycemia and early onset diabetes. They may also have a tendency to food allergies. When they worry, their tummies can get upset. Worry is one of Earths' main emotions.

How to Help Your Earth Child

- ♥ **Give them important jobs around the house.** They love and want to help out. Giving them tasks will make them feel special. Acknowledge them whenever you can. Earth kids can hold a secret resentment if they aren't thanked enough.

- ♥ **Encourage taking more risks.** Earth children stay in their comfort zones throughout their lives. In their youth, help them to stretch beyond their boundaries while staying safe.

- ♥ **Teach them healthy bonding.** Earth and Fire children can be extra cuddly and affectionate with their friends and family because they feel so much love. Teach them about boundaries and appropriate behaviors in certain contexts.

- ♥ **Give them time to process change.** Prepare Earth children well in advance for change so they have enough time to process it. Telling

284

them about the day's activities in the morning or as soon as possible will also keep the drama out of your day.

- **Help them identify their emotions.** Earth kids are so empathetic that they may lose sight of their *own* emotions. Therefore, they may find it hard to know what's going on inside of themselves. Check in with them and help them to get balanced.

- **Help them manage their digestive issues.** The stomach and spleen are the two organs that govern the Earth element. When Earth children are stressed-out, their digestions can suffer. An Eden Medicine Exercise, the Butterfly Hug, is very good to soothe this stress.

- **Help them separate fantasy from reality.** Earth children believe in fairy tales. Their first serious intimate relationship can lead to severe heartbreak if the fairy tale doesn't come true. It may take them an extra-long time to recover. Read them lots of different tales, not just the ones with happy endings, and have discussions about the stories afterward.

- **Empower them to develop self-love.** Earth children want to please others before themselves. They are always seeking approval rather than developing self-confidence. Help them strengthen their love for themselves.

285

The Earth Child Overview

Earth Child Archetypes	Mommy and Daddy's Little Helper, the Daydreamer
Animal Archetype	Deer or Cow (gentle, they take their time)
Earth's Superpowers	They have a compassionate, considerate, and caring attitude toward everyone and everything in life.
Earth's Fears	They are scared that their reality will change.
Earth's Challenges	They can suffer and worry for others too much. They may suppress their anger, and so others may never know there's a problem.
Stress Responses	They worry too much about things before they happen. They can have confused emotions and scattered thinking.
Earth's Needs	They need to bring more love and self-esteem to themselves.
Physical Reactions	Digestive problems, overeating, irritable bowel syndrome, diabetes, gas, sensitive gums.
Earth's Lessons	Earths need to have compassion for themselves, just as they would for their best friend.

The Earth Parent	Ultimate Mother Earth and Gentle Father. Yet they can also be helicopter parents, hovering too close and micromanaging their child's needs.
Earth Movement	An easy beat, like 4/4 time. Circle dancing with a group.
Earth Exercise	Butterfly Hug

Earth Exercise: Butterfly Hug

A big lesson for Earth children is remembering to love themselves. In this exercise, they hold both sides of their body in the Butterfly Hug. Their arms are wrapped around spleen and liver. The spleen governs the Earth element and is the metabolizer of emotional energies; the liver governs the Wood element and in Chinese medicine liver-dominant people are usually hard on themselves. Rocking the spleen and liver can bring balance and calm to the nervous system and the energy body.

FIG. 1   FIG. 2

1. Open your arms wide to both sides as if you are a beautiful butterfly or a peacock showing off your tail feathers. Breathe in (Fig. 1).
2. Give yourself a big hug with your wings, wrapping them tightly around your waist. Breathe out (Fig. 2).

288

3. With your arms around yourself, sway side to side as if you're rocking a baby, and say, "Shhhhhh. . . ." Think of something good you did for someone else and give that love back to yourself.

4. Repeat, opening up your arms wide again and then switch arms to wrap them in a big hug once more.

Ideas for the Classroom. Establishing community with circle dancing, singing, or playing musical instruments together is a nice connection to have with your class. Bringing animals into the classroom or creating little gardening or cooking stations helps stabilize the Earth energy in your classroom. Such activities also delight the Earth and Fire children by strengthening social connections. Music: folk dance music, African call-and-response singing, fairy-tale songs in 4/4 time, like "Puff the Magic Dragon."

The Metal Child

Autumn's Child Is Metal

A smart and intellectual boy, Jacob loved school and loved to learn. He always got good grades, finished all of his projects, and challenged his teachers, not by acting out but by asking questions so academic that they'd have to do research to answer him. They loved the challenge, and Jacob loved his teachers. Jacob was an encyclopedia of information, always focused on the details of every project or subject he was learning about.

Jacob made his parents proud, but he was quite different from them. Even though he loved them, he sometimes felt that he'd been born into the wrong family. He found his mom and dad too laid-back in their daily schedules. Sometimes he cleaned up after them because the disorder bothered him so much. Dad was a struggling musician and Mom was a waitress; they had two children to support, so money was tight. Jacob longed for more opportunities like the other kids in school, who had their very own computers. Keeping to himself, he spent his time in the computer room at school and became known as somewhat of a geek.

Jacob's mom and dad knew that their son excelled. They really wanted to send him to a better school that would meet his needs, but they just couldn't afford to move or pay for private school. Jacob felt despondent, his needs unmet. He had breathing problems that turned into asthma. Carrying around an inhaler didn't help him overcome his label as a nerd.

Metal is autumn, the time when the leaves fall off the trees and many life-forms prepare for winter hibernation. Metal is the last element in the wheel and it relates to endings, death, and deep reflection. It is also about contemplation. Metal children are the kids who are asking questions about the universe and beyond. They commit themselves to projects and they see them through to the end. Detail is part of their language. They will tell you, in great detail, what they observe, what is needed, and how to make it better. They are often long-winded.

Metal kids are perfectionists, from lining up their toys and putting them into categories to diligently working on homework assignments. They even show the teacher better ways to do things. Proud Metal children love to see their accomplishments recognized in high grades, awards, and certificates. They like to see where they came from and where they're going. They appreciate charts that outline their achievements and mark their hard work while previewing their upcoming endeavors.

Metal kids are little scientists always concentrating seriously on their work. When working on a project, they are more detailed and precise than most children. They like to take things apart just to figure out how to put them back together again. They like puzzles; they like to solve mysteries. They're little wizards who can logically transform ideas into realistic goals. Metal children gather valuable information to serve them in life. Scientific facts and research thrill them, and they'll be reciting newly learned terms to you with the aplomb of a college professor.

Metal children usually grow into long limbs and lanky bodies. They can feel awkward in their own skin, may lack boundary awareness, and may appear physically uncoordinated, so they're often picked on socially.

291

They're always trying to maintain a sense of order. While working on their projects, they set high standards of excellence. When they see that something's wrong, they won't relax until order is restored. They work relentlessly, with no regard for the passing of time or the hour of the day. They stay focused until they are done.

Metals are the most serious of students, always glued to their computers or deeply involved in reading and research. They have great minds, and learn quickly. But at times they may also act like know-it-alls. To make things worse, Metal kids are so focused on their brilliant ideas that they may dismiss the opinions of others. They are dry in their own opinions and although their straightforwardness may seem like criticism, really they're trying to understand and put everything into logical perspective.

Metal kids get good grades and are motivated by excellence. They love to please their parents and teachers. When they know that they've displeased an authority figure, they can feel very small.

They can be picky and unusual with their food, not liking certain items to touch other items on their plates, for example. They crave spicy flavors. As teenagers and young adults, they can become compulsive in their eating habits and may develop body-image disorders.

Metal children tend to have neat and orderly rooms without a lot of clutter. Disorder disturbs them. Their rooms are their sanctuaries where they enjoy spending time alone. They keep to themselves, often without any friends, although they may yearn for companions, and this private yearning may cause them some grief.

When they do play with other kids, they like board games that require some strategy. When other kids break the rules, Metals can get frustrated, so to keep the peace, they might recite and repeat the rules stoically and methodically. Metal kids don't like messy activities, like finger painting or splashing in puddles. They are usually interested in outer space and deciphering theory, patterns, and codes, so, telescopes and models of the solar system are great gifts for Metals, as are science kits, magic-trick sets, and puzzles.

The lungs govern Metal, and these children can have issues with breathing and asthma, especially under stress. Many of the kids being born today have allergies, but Metal children are especially prone to them. They can develop additional allergies to foods or materials in their surroundings. Skin issues and eruptions can also flare up in times of trauma. In the teen years, anguish over difficult transitions can be expressed in the skin as acne.

How to Help Your Metal Child

- ♥ **Give them structure with consistency.** Metal kids feel safe in familiar routines and schedules. Give them a sense of safety and support by providing boundaries.

- ♥ **Balance their time on the computer.** Metal kids can get too serious, even addicted to the computer, especially with video games. Balance this out by getting them to take breaks and connect to nature outside.

- ♥ **Encourage them to play more.** Support them to have fun and not be so serious. Tell them to just be kids! Use humor and silliness to help them laugh at themselves. Set up play dates with other kids with similar interests.

293

♥ **Praise them.** Specific compliments will go further in helping them to improve than giving general praise. Especially do not point out their faults in public. This can be devastating.

♥ **Metal kids need to move.** Because Metals spend too much time in their heads, they miss out on normal aspects of childhood. Enroll them in stretch, yoga, or swimming classes. Being in water helps them to find flow by bringing movement into their lower limbs and helping them to overcome their physical awkwardness.

294

The Metal Child Overview

Metal Child Archetypes	The Scientist, the Wizard
Animal Archetype	Giraffe (from high up they're able to see the fray)
Metal's Superpowers	They usually get good grades and focus and apply themselves well.
Metal's Fears	Not having enough time for their projects. Not being the wisest or smartest person in the room.
Metal's Challenges	They can dismiss others easily and separate themselves from friends.
Stress Responses	They can be dismissive, withdrawn, and obstinate. (Don't let them go too far down this path.)
Metal's Needs	To play more, have fun, and just be a kid.
Physical Reactions	Asthma, breathing problems, colds, skin and hair issues, hypersensitivities, poor bowel movements.
Metal's Lessons	Metals need to let go, surrender to the situation, and lighten up.
The Metal Parent	Teacher Parent. Every moment is another learning opportunity—they are rarely just fun and enjoyable.

295

(continued)

Metal Movement	Breathing, stretching, yoga, and meditation. Swimming may help them to be more in the flow.
Metal Exercise	Hiawatha's Arrow

Metal Exercise: Hiawatha's Arrow

This exercise is for the lung meridian, letting go, and moving on. This helps Metal children to not live in their minds so much. It increases their inner strength and helps them let go.

FIG. 1   FIG. 2   FIG. 3

1. Breathe in and reach one hand behind you and up to the sky. Pretend to receive your own personal arrow from the gods and goddesses (Fig. 1).
2. Breathe out as you lunge forward to meet your other arm stretched out in front of you. Pretend to string the arrow into your bow as you see a target in front of you (Fig. 2).
3. Breathe in as you draw your arrow back, bending your elbow as you pass your lungs. Keep the other arm straight in front of you (Fig. 3).

297

FIG. 4   FIG. 5   FIG. 6

4. Breathe out as you let your arrow go, bringing your back arm to meet the straight arm in front. Step both feet together (Figs. 4, 5).

5. Breathe in as you open up your arms like an airplane, to either side of your body, as you stand up on your tippy-toes (Fig. 5).

6. Breathe out as your arms come back to your sides and your heels come back to the ground.

7. Repeat on the other side.

Ideas for the Classroom. Do yoga, meditation, and breath work with Metal kids. Pretend you're all a flock of birds and dance and fly together. Their arms become wings as they breathe through the movements. Have them perch on their nests and feel the stillness as they stop. Music: light, classical music or none.

Our children need our guidance to help them grow into empowered and balanced adults who respect one another and live with integrity. Using the Five Elements to interact and guide your children will help us create a more peaceful, thriving planet and healthier generations hereafter. Have fun!

Helpful Resources

Here is a short list of ways to get connected and learn more about the Five Elements:

https://www.facebook.com/DondiDahlinFanPage. Join me on Facebook as we discuss the Five Elements.

www.LearnTheFiveElements.com. Learn more about the Five Elements and keep up-to-date on radio and TV shows where I delve deep into the Five Elements and Energy Medicine.

www.LearnEnergyMedicine.com. You can spend hours at this website learning more about Eden Energy Medicine, the Five Elements, and the work of my mom, Donna Eden.

Donna Eden, *Energy Medicine: Balancing Your Body's Energies for Optimal Health, Joy, and Vitality.* (New York: Penguin, 2008). This book is considered the bible of energy medicine. It has changed many lives and as one review said, "A must-have book for anyone who is breathing."

Lauren Walker, *Energy Medicine Yoga: Amplify the Healing Power of Your Yoga Practice* (Sounds True: 2014). Lauren combines Eden Energy Medicine and yoga for a powerful practice that beginner and advanced yogis will find intriguing and exciting.

Harriet Beinfield and Efrem Korngold, *Between Heaven and Earth: A Guide to Chinese Medicine*. (New York: Ballantine, 1992). This is a time-tested book on the Five Elements and one that many people use for deep study in health and wellness. For years I borrowed my mom's dog-eared copy, until I finally bought my own. It will help you understand your health and your elements in a profound way.

Charles A. Moss, *Power of the Five Elements: The Chinese Medicine Path to Healthy Aging and Stress Resistance*. (Berkeley, CA: North Atlantic Books, 2010). This is a very useful book that will help all ages, but especially those wanting to be vital and healthy as they get older.

Cheryl Schwartz, *Four Paws, Five Directions: A Guide to Chinese Medicine for Cats and Dogs* (Berkeley, CA: Celestial Arts, 1996). An enlightening, humorous, and comprehensive handbook for pet care using the Five Elements system.

ACKNOWLEDGMENTS

YEARS AGO I LIVED ALONE in a small cottage on the beach and I dreamed of writing a book. Surge forward twenty years and I am writing a book while raising my five-year-old, homeschooling, and working full-time. It is a whole different ball game than those days of solitude at the ocean and it would have been almost impossible to do without the incredible amount of support I receive.

Mom, you taught me the Five Elements. You continue to teach me love, acceptance, generosity, and compassion. You see my heart, you feel my soul, you make me feel safe, and you "get" me. My kindest and most loving parts came from me watching you all my life and using you as my highest teacher. You have always trusted me, and have made me feel like I am a great human being. You have taught me to celebrate moments and to eat dessert first, metaphorically and literally. You have made my life an infinitely more meaningful, compassionate, and healthy one, when I might have otherwise become a stuck Wood. You always tell me I am so smart and wise. *You make me feel smart and wise!*

Mom and David, you two have lived your life being "heart-centered" decades before the term became popular. You are the ultimate role models for generosity and compassion and I love working for you! The support you give me with my career, with writing, and with all of my endeavors keeps me going. I so appreciate that you value and honor my hard work and make me feel that every bit of it is worth it. Plus, you are the "dream team" of grandparents to Tiernan Ray.

Tanya, thank you for making this book complete by writing the all-important Afterword, which will benefit so many people. Thank you for our shared laughter—

there is a magical and healing laugh that we experience that I have never experienced with anyone else. We seem to read each other's minds, hear each other's jokes, and laugh so hard that we fall down on the floor with no sound coming out of our mouths, only to catch our breaths minutes later, howling until we cannot laugh anymore. Our bond transcends words. My hope for you, in this lifetime, is that you finally get how incredibly beautiful and amazing you are. I love you, Tanya. Jeff, thank you for loving Tanya unconditionally, and also being my buddy.

Everyone needs a mate who says, "Take some time off. Go write. I will take care of our son. Put everything out of your mind and go do what you need to do. Get this book done." Thank you, Roger. You are supportive of me and the greatest father in the world to our son, Tiernan. You are the father that every child deserves to have. Our union is unconventional and yet our bond and our love is undeniable.

I have never known a love like my love with Tiernan Ray. Tiernan, you are my greatest testament to a life well lived and decisions made wisely. We know each other through and through and I often feel like we are one. Before you came along I had a void, but I had no idea what was missing and I didn't know how to fill it. I had a successful career traveling around the world, a glamorous life, and a wonderful cottage on the beach in California. I would sit and look at the Pacific Ocean and wonder, "What is this hole I am feeling and what could possibly fill it?" It was you. At forty years old, I found my life made complete by you; you filled the void, and now I am whole.

Thank you to everyone who was involved in the production of this book! The Tarcher family: Joel Fotinos, Sara Carder, Joanna Ng, Brianna Yamashita, Angela Januzzi, and Cathy Serpico—I enjoy our moments together in New York and I am so very proud to shout to the world that I am a Tarcher author! Videographers: Jill Stevens and Elizabeth Watts of Hip Chicks Create—having you as my personal videographers was a boon for this project (I know it was a chore to film on location in Hawaii and Miami). Photographers Rick Unis and Bernadette Unis-Johnston—you

302

are very good at wrangling all of the kids and adults to make awesome photos. Kelly Notaras and Joelle Hann, you gave me valuable advice and you steered me in the right directions. Jack Canfield and Steve Harrison, you believed in me and also motivated, inspired, and pushed me to stay on course and made this book better as a result.

Innersource staff, you are always there when I need you, even at a moment's notice. You are the best team in the world! Thank you for picking up the pieces during my intense days of writing.

To the Eden Energy Medicine Certification Program Faculty and community, I thank you for the warm smiles, hugs, and votes of confidence! I always appreciate your support at classes and workshops around the world, as well as on social media.

There are friends who have cheerleaded me through the years of my dance, acting, and speaking career from Los Angeles to Miami, Jordan to Dubai. Now you all are cheerleading me through my writing career. The positive phone calls, the uplifting e-mails, the funny texts, and the pats on the shoulder have helped me move forward toward my lofty goals. My heart and soul thank you!

Thank you to the celebrities and well-known people I have mentioned in this book. I have attempted to tell what elements you are, based on having worked with you or studied you, but I may have captured your public persona more than your private one. The truth is that many of you are a mix of elements, and you may be stronger in elements that we don't see when you are behind closed doors and not in the public eye. I've made my best effort to describe your elements within the limits of what I know of you.

I thank my lucky starts every day. I am a blessed woman to have so many people love me and enthusiastically support me. I will never take it for granted.

303

ABOUT THE AUTHOR

***THE FIVE ELEMENTS* IS DONDI'S** second book. She cowrote *The Little Book of Energy Medicine* with her mother, Energy Medicine pioneer Donna Eden. Dondi is an award-winning public speaker and internationally acclaimed dancer and actor in television, film, and stage and has been a member of the Screen Actors Guild since 1991. She has taught the Five Elements with her sister, Titanya Dahlin, at the renowned Omega Institute in New York since 2001, as well as other workshops and conferences around the world. Dondi lives in California and homeschools her son in a 1904 Victorian Folk house that she fought for two years to get historically designated and on the Historic Register of San Diego.

ACKNOWLEDGMENTS

CREDITS

Photography by Narrative Images Photography: www.narrativeimagesphoto.com

Models:
Yerdanos Ali
Dondi Dahlin
Tiernan Devenyns Dahlin
Kai Dornfeld
David Fleer
Rose Harris
Gryphon Stroud Mellor
Nichola Jade Mellor
Miranda Muse
Marguerite Spooner
Sophia Tabrizi